CN00793418

The BEGGARSTAFF *POSTERS*

The BEGGARSTAFF *POSTERS*

THE WORK OF
JAMES PRYDE AND WILLIAM NICHOLSON

Colin
CAMPBELL

(*Frontispiece*) William Nicholson outside Chaucer's House, Woodstock, c. 1898/9. James Pryde, who holds Nicholson's son Ben in his arms, can be seen through the window.

BARRIE & JENKINS
LONDON

First published in Great Britain in 1990 by
Barrie & Jenkins Ltd
20 Vauxhall Bridge Road
London SW1V 2SA

British Library Cataloguing in Publication Data
Campbell, Colin
The Beggarstaff posters: the work of James Pryde and
William Nicholson.
1. English posters. Nicholson, William. Pryde, James.
Nicholson, William & Pryde, James
I. Title
769.92′2

ISBN 0–7126–2079–6

Designed by David Fordham
Typeset by Wyvern Typesetting Limited
Printed by BAS Printers Limited,
Over Wallop, Hampshire

Contents

This book is dedicated to
the memory of my father

Robert Campbell

Foreword

hen James Pryde and William Nicholson made their début as poster designers at the Westminster Aquarium exhibition of 1894, they did so under their chosen pseudonym of 'J. & W. Beggarstaff'. The name confused some of the reviewers (the journals of the day are scattered with references to Messrs Biggerstaff, Baggerstaff and Bickerstaff), but there was little doubt in the critics' minds about the importance of the work of this new duo. The two young artists' contributions to the exhibition were praised for both their formal beauty and their effectiveness as advertisements, and a tremendous future was predicted for them.

The enthusiastic verdict of the nineteenth century has been endorsed by that of the twentieth. Although the Beggarstaffs did not have much commercial success during their short period of collaboration, they have undoubtedly had a significant influence on the evolution of ideas about the form and function of posters. Their use of silhouettes composed of pure, flat tints, the attention they paid to their lettering and their emphasis on economy in both image and caption were a source of inspiration when the pictorial placard finally came into its own during the 1920s; and the artists are thus rightly regarded as pioneers of the modern advertisement.

How is it that two designers with such an unchallenged reputation have not hitherto been the subject of a serious study? One of the reasons is that few of the Beggarstaffs' designs were actually reproduced and used on the hoardings. If the preliminary designs for unpublished works had survived, this would of course have mattered less. Unfortunately, however, several such designs have been lost, and it is rarely possible to reconstruct their appearance. The few designs that do survive are often in a poor state of preservation, and many of the extant works also present problems where chronology is concerned. As if this was not discouraging enough, source material is disappointingly scarce and uninformative. The artists themselves said relatively little about their work, and the difficulties of finding a language appropriate to the new art form are all too evident in the critical writings of the Beggarstaffs' contemporaries. In later years, when attention switched from the posters of Pryde and Nicholson to the two artists' paintings, writers who knew one or other of them, such as James Laver and Marguerite Steen, missed opportunities to record details of this remarkable partnership.

The principal aims of the present volume are, firstly, to catalogue and illustrate the Beggarstaff *oeuvre*, and, secondly, to discuss – as far as the available material allows – the various technical and formal aspects, such as materials, techniques, creative procedures, formal characteristics and stylistic development. Posters, even more than paintings, cannot be considered outside the context of their time, and so I have also paid some attention to the circumstances which led to their creation, the influence on the Beggarstaffs of other artists, and the critical reactions of contemporaries. In a more general way, I have attempted to place certain products of the partnership in the framework of the social and cultural changes that created the conditions for the poster 'boom' of the 1890s.

A book which sets out to fill this gap in the history of English art must obviously pay due regard to those designs which were put to a commercial use; but I have tried not to emphasise published works at the expense of designs which, for one reason or another, never reached the hoardings. After all, creations such as the unpublished designs for Sir Henry Irving are among the finest of the Beggarstaffs' efforts; and many people would agree with McKnight Kauffer's statement that the famous *Don Quixote* was the 'best poster ever'. It has also seemed appropriate to extend discussion of the *oeuvre* to include other work in which Pryde and Nicholson collaborated between 1894 and 1899: decorative panels, book illustration and painted signboards. Although the posters that Pryde and Nicholson produced on their own account after the dissolution of the Beggarstaff partnership are outside the scope of this study, I have briefly referred to these works in the concluding section of the introductory text. As for the subject of the Beggarstaffs' influence on other poster designers, that is best left to the authors of future studies on the individual designers in question.

I would like to express my gratitude to a number of people who have freely given their help during the period I have spent writing this book. Among those who supplied photographs, allowed the reproduction of works of art in their possession, answered enquiries or helped in other ways are Messrs Abbott & Holder; David Anderson; Mrs Elizabeth Banks; Dr Judith Bronkhurst; the staff of the Print Department, Christie's; Mrs E. I. Edwards (Archives Section, Technical Library, Rowntree Mackintosh); Jim Emmett (Emmett Publishing Ltd); Mrs Rowland Eustace; Rosemary Evison (National Portrait Gallery); Christopher Gilbert (Leeds City Art Galleries); John Grimond; H. A. Hanley (County Archivist, Buckingham County Council); Stephen G. Herrick; Derek Hudson; Anna Jackson (Theatre Museum, London); Dr Hermann Kleinstück; Brian North Lee; Andrew McIntosh Patrick (The Fine Art Society, London); Peter Miall (The National Trust); Dr Michael Pidgley (Exeter College of Art and Design); Timothy Rogers (Bodleian Library, Oxford); Stanley Scott; Peyton Skipwith (The Fine Art Society); Mrs Anthony Thomas (Ellen Terry Memorial Museum, Tenterden); Peter Walne (County Archivist, Hertfordshire County Council); and Mrs Margaret Weare (Ellen Terry Memorial Museum). I am particularly grateful to Mr Timothy Nicholson for the interest he has shown in this project, and for the assistance he has given on a number of occasions. Finally, a special word of thanks is due to Margaret Timmers (Department of Designs, Prints and Drawings, Victoria and Albert Museum, London), who read the draft typescript and made a number of helpful suggestions.

COLIN CAMPBELL

The BEGGARSTAFF *POSTERS*

Note on the Text and Illustrations

A number of the early sources refer to James Pryde and William Nicholson as 'the Beggarstaff Brothers', and this term has since become common in modern references to the artists. Nicholson himself is reported (in an article in the January 1896 issue of *The Idler*) to have said that he and Pryde 'hit upon the idea of calling ourselves the brothers Beggarstaff', but he later protested against the use of the word 'brothers', and at all other times during the period of their collaboration the two artists referred to themselves as either 'J. & W. Beggarstaff' or 'Beggarstaffs'. The pseudonyms that the artists themselves preferred have been employed in the text of this book.

The word 'design', which has a variety of meanings in the art historian's vocabulary, is generally used here to describe an image (usually composed of pieces of cut and pasted paper) in which the composition of a poster is worked out prior to publication. Where the original titles of works of art are unknown, the titles preferred by the authors of the first published descriptions have usually been cited. Where the exact date of a work is unknown, such forms as 1894/5 (which means 'at some point in 1894 or 1895') or c. 1894/5 ('probably dating from 1894 or 1895, but there is a possibility that the work may be from before or after these years') have been used. Some bibliographical references are given in the footnotes at the end of the introductory text. Details of other publications by cited writers can be found in the Bibliography at the end of the book. Where a cited author is represented in the Bibliography by more than one book or article, the reader is referred to the relevant publication by a reference to the year in which the text in question appeared. Where two or more publications by a single author date from the same year, they are distinguished from each other by references to the order in which they appear in the Bibliography. For example, 'Macfall (1895/1)' refers to the first of Haldane Macfall's 1895 articles, and 'Macfall (1895/2)' refers to the second.

In the case of the *Girl reading*, the *Roundhead*, the *Cinderella* and the last of the three *Don Quixote* designs, colour plates have had to be based on reproductions made during the period of the Beggarstaff partnership, as the originals do not survive. In the case of the *Harper's Magazine* bill, examples of the printed poster survive, but they are usually in such a poor state of preservation that it seemed preferable to use, once again, an accurate contemporary reproduction. A colour transparency of a fine example of the printed *Cinderella* poster which is in the Museum für Kunst und Gewerbe, Hamburg, was ordered, but unfortunately there was no time left in which to make alternative arrangements when the museum ran into difficulties in photographing this large poster, and the work has therefore had to be reproduced in black and white.

References to the illustrations are given in square brackets (roman numerals refer to colour plates). Measurements, where known, are given in inches, with height preceding width.

James Pryde and William Nicholson

AMES FERRIER PRYDE (1866–1941) WAS BORN IN EDINBURGH, the only son in a family of six children. Two aspects of his Scottish background were to influence his life as an artist. The first of these was his native city, memories of whose architecture haunted his paintings for many years. The second was the theatre. Jimmy's father, for some years headmaster of Edinburgh Ladies College, was an ardent admirer of the great actor-manager Henry Irving, who became an intimate friend. Ellen Terry, who appeared in many of Irving's Lyceum productions, was also revered. Derek Hudson recorded in his fine biography of Dr Pryde's artist son that Pryde senior's devotion to theatre was shared by his entire family. Indeed, the cult of Irving reached such heights in the household that, after one occasion on which the actor had dined at their home in Fettes Row, Mrs Pryde was heard to say that the glass from which the great man had drunk must never be washed. Excited by talk of plays and players, young Jimmy Pryde's imagination was soon captured by the romance of the stage. His youthful admiration for Irving, inherited from his parents, was later to be of considerable importance for the Beggarstaff partnership.

After studying at the Royal Scottish Academy School, Jimmy decided to continue his artistic education at the Académie Julian in Paris. Here, students of many different nationalities spent their weekdays painting models from life and their Sundays competing in the creation of an *esquisse* or painting of a subject from the Bible. Unfortunately, the teaching was indifferent, and the enormous ground-floor atelier in which the students worked was apparently overcrowded and smelt of tobacco, bodies and stove oil. It was a dismal place, and the fastidious young Scot left France after only three months. Jimmy returned to Edinburgh, and after a spell there decided to try his luck in London. Before long, he began to make a modest reputation for himself as a pastellist working in the manner of Whistler.

William Newzam Prior Nicholson (1872–1949) was born at Newark-on-Trent, Nottinghamshire, the youngest child of an industrialist who specialised in the manufacture of agricultural machinery. Young William never showed any interest in joining the family firm. At the age of twelve he began receiving lessons from a local artist named William Cubley, and four years later he enrolled at the school of art which the German-born Hubert Herkomer had opened at Bushey, Hertfordshire.

Herkomer, who made a fortune from portraits and sentimental narrative pictures, was a conventional and uninspiring teacher; but he was an artist with an impressive range of interests that included print-making, film-making and scenic art. He enjoyed writing music-plays, which he regarded as having an importance for his students as lessons in 'picture-making'. These plays, which allowed Herkomer to indulge his interest in theatrical experiments of various kinds, were staged in a theatre erected in the grounds of the art school. One of the triumphs of a production prepared during the period of William's stay at Bushey was a large harvest moon with a soft, mysterious halo that rose with almost imperceptible motion, the light emitted from it gradually increasing as the object ascended into a darkening sky. The subtle light effects of this moon were created by means of a varying electric current [1]. Experiments such as these must have made an impression on William, whose life-long passion for the theatre was first aroused at this time.

A MOONLIGHTER AT BUSHEY.

Professor H-rk-m-r, A.R.A., instructing Master Henry Irving and Master Gussie Harris how to illuminate "The Inconstant Moon." (*"The Moon was not like the Moon ordinarily seen on the stage."—Vide general journalistic opinion on the "Herkomer Opera."*)

1 Linley Sambourne, *A Moonlighter at Bushey* (Hubert Herkomer lecturing Sir Augustus Harris and Henry Irving). Sambourne's cartoon refers to Herkomer's lecture on 'Scenic Art' at the Avenue Theatre in January 1892.

One day, not long after Nicholson's arrival at Bushey, the portentous atmosphere of Herkomer's life class was disturbed by a flock of geese which a high-spirited student had discovered on an adjacent common and driven into the building. The girl responsible turned out to be Mabel, the youngest of the Pryde family. Like her brother James, Mabel had artistic talent, and had managed to persuade her parents to let her study painting. 'Prydie', whom Max Beerbohm later described as looking like the result of an intrigue between Milton and the Mona Lisa, attracted the young man from Newark, and the two became close friends. During their conversations, William heard a great deal about Mabel's brother Jimmy – who, in due course, arrived at Bushey, elegantly dressed in his Scotch tweeds. For a time, Jimmy shared lodgings with his sister, and William, charmed by the way this gifted and amusing man talked with such easy familiarity about Paris, Whistler and the modern Scottish painters, got to know him well.

Apart from a liking for beautifully tailored clothes, Pryde and Nicholson had little in common where appearances were concerned. The former was tall and inclined to corpulence, while the latter was small and thin. But the differences were more than superficial: the dignified bearing and apparent self-confidence that Pryde possessed even as a young man contrasted markedly with the more diffident manner that contemporaries remarked on in Nicholson, six years his junior. There were disparities of temperament, too, between the sensitive, somewhat detached Nicholson and his more ebullient, convivial companion. These differences seemed to manifest themselves in their respective approaches to their work: Nicholson restlessly creative; Pryde more leisurely – perhaps, on occasions, even idle.

There is no doubt that at this stage in their relationship Pryde was the dominant personality, and his contemptuous attitude towards Herkomer's teaching now kindled in Nicholson a capacity for independence of thought in artistic matters that was to lead to the younger man's premature departure from Bushey. On one of the occasions when it was Nicholson's turn to pose the studio model, he asked a woman from the village to sit with a large black umbrella open behind her head. Having completed his own sketch of this model, Nicholson left the studio, only to find, on his return, Herkomer fuming over what he took to be a piece of 'Whistlerian impudence'. Sensing the subversive influence of Pryde, Herkomer gave Nicholson notice of dismissal for 'bad attendance and bad work'. Marguerite Steen tells us that the note crossed with his pupil's letter of resignation.

Prompted by the example of Jimmy Pryde and countless other young artists, Nicholson set off for France. It was 1889, and with the Exposition Universelle Paris had much to offer. A feast of modern French painting was on view at the Luxembourg Museum and elsewhere, and many special exhibitions (including Ernest Maindron's survey of French posters) had been mounted. The classes at the Académie Julian, on the other hand, were as much a disappointment to Nicholson as they had been to Pryde, and after six months in the French capital he returned to England. A studio was built for him in the garden of his parents' Newark home, and he settled down to follow his own path. However, he did not remain in the Midlands for long. By 1892 provincial life had become irksome to a youth who had already tasted independence, and Nicholson headed for London. He had already begun to exhibit at the New English Art Club, and in the spring of 1892 an additional reason for going south was a visit to the retrospective show of Whistler's work at the Goupil Gallery.

Another of London's attractions was Mabel Pryde. Following Dr Pryde's resignation from his teaching post, he and his family had moved to London – where they would have the Lyceum and other London theatres close at hand – and Nicholson took the opportunity of calling on Jimmy Pryde's sister at her parents' new home in Woburn Place. Nicholson had not previously encountered the family *en masse*. The Prydes were not just eccentric, but opinionated, too; and Steen remarked that it 'must have seemed a very odd household to William, after the gentle, well-bred, well-mannered atmosphere of his own. Unaccustomed to argument, to the violent expression of violent views, he found it enormously stimulating.' Mabel's mother was against marriage; and so, after a courtship conducted largely, it seems, among the coalsacks in the cellar of the Prydes' Bloomsbury home, the couple married in secret at Ruislip on 25 April 1893.

2 The Eight Bells, Denham, Buckinghamshire, in the 1890s. From a photograph in *The Idler*, January 1896.

After the honeymoon, the young couple moved into a former public house known as the Eight Bells at Denham, Buckinghamshire [2]. Now part of Greater London, Denham was then a small, old-fashioned, typical English village in an idyllic rural setting. Shortly after the move, Mabel's brother arrived. The Eight Bells was not very spacious, but Jimmy was not deterred by this, and his visit lasted, on and off, for nearly two years. Hudson points out in his biography of Pryde that in 1893 the young artist was urgently in need of encouragement and support. 'He had made his mark among his fellow artists in Edinburgh and

London, but had had no popular success. Though he had done some illustrations for books – two shadowy, suggestive wash drawings for Wilhelm Hauff's *The Little Glass Man* were published by Cassell in 1893 – his existence must have been on a hand-to-mouth basis. Unbusinesslike, charming, vain, lazy, he needed, above all, someone who would take him in hand and show him that it was worth persevering seriously with his enormous artistic talent.' Instinctively, he looked to his favourite sister and her husband for this support.

3 Photograph of Ellen Terry and Edward Gordon Craig in Charles Reade's comedy *Nance Oldfield*.

One evening, returning on the train from London to his adopted home at Denham, Pryde ran into the actor Edward Gordon Craig [3]. They had met once before – at the Lyceum Theatre – and Pryde discovered that the recently married Craig was now living at nearby Uxbridge, with his wife May, in a cottage rented from his mother, Ellen Terry. Following this encounter, Craig and his wife visited the Nicholsons and Jimmy Pryde at the Eight Bells from time to time, and before the birth of the Nicholsons' first child, Ben, in April 1894, they stayed there for a while. These were relatively carefree days, and Craig later recalled a 'beautiful tale of a very English cottage and lots of fresh air and sunshine and old Jimmy fast asleep upstairs and the Kid [Nicholson] and his active bubbling wit'. The conversation of this group of friends centred round a multiplicity of shared interests: old woodcuts; early Italian paintings; Honoré Daumier; the etchings of the seventeenth-century French printmaker Jacques Callot; and the historical novels of Alexandre Dumas. It was at this time that Nicholson gave Craig a few informal lessons in the art of engraving boxwood, a technique which the latter soon put to use in a series of charming and accomplished bookplates. One of the finest of these, done a few years later, was for Pryde.

Above all, they talked about the theatre. As often as possible, the Nicholsons would go up to London to see productions at the Lyceum (where Craig was engaged) and elsewhere. Pryde went with them. As a boy, Jimmy had once offered his services to Henry Irving (only to be sent back to his father with a note of thanks), and he still hankered after a career on the stage.

In consideration of his long-standing friendship with Dr Pryde, Henry Irving always sent Pryde's daughter Mabel and her husband first-night seats, with a little personal note. Marguerite Steen recorded that William and Mabel, who were incapable of saving a penny for practical purposes, kept two boxes, one labelled 'FOR BOOTS', which was always empty, and the other 'THE IRVING FUND', to be used on Lyceum first nights. 'A "command" to the Lyceum' wrote Steen, 'meant a tramp along country lanes (no question of affording a carriage), Mabel's gown held up out of the mud, William guarding the immaculacy of his solitary dress-shirt, specially laundered for the occasion.' They were always invited to go behind for the first-night party, and this meant returning to Uxbridge on a midnight train and tramping out again to the Eight Bells in the dark. 'On one such night,' wrote Steen, 'it snowed, and they read in the morning papers that some of the bus-drivers had frozen to death on their boxes. Devotion to the theatre could go no farther.' Craig's mother, Ellen Terry, also showed the Nicholsons hospitality, on one occasion asking them to lunch at Barkston Gardens. After lunch they played spillikins, at which, apparently, Henry Irving cheated.

In the summer of 1894, Gordon Craig left the Lyceum to join the W. S. Hardy Shakespeare Company, which was at that time preparing for a tour of the provinces with a production of *Hamlet*, beginning at Hereford. Craig was to play the title role in this production. It was a milestone in his career as an actor, and his thoughts turned to the question of how his performance should be publicised.

He was quite capable of producing a poster himself (he had designed bills for earlier touring productions in which he had taken part), but on this occasion it was decided that the task should be given to his two friends.

THE PICTORIAL POSTER IN ENGLAND

OR A LARGE PART OF THE NINETEENTH CENTURY, POSTERS HAD been of the letterpress only kind. The art historian and critic M. H. Spielmann wrote that as late as the middle of the century art remained 'unsmirched, save by Rowland's "incomparable" Macassar Oil, beloved of Byron, and Warren's Nubian Blacking. The former showed us the interesting but unconvincing spectacle of a lady covered from head to foot with a luxuriant growth of hair obtained through a course of judicious loyalty to Mrs Rowland; and the latter, the delight of a negro grinning at the reflection of his face in a Wellington boot to which he had applied the splendour that lay hid in the blacking-bottle. And that was practically the sum of English poster art.'

The first work of any importance in the history of the pictorial poster in England is Frederick Walker's famous black-and-white design for a stage adaptation of Wilkie Collins's *The Woman in White* (1871). Unfortunately, Walker's startlingly original design, which was engraved on wood by W. H. Hooper, went largely unnoticed and had little influence. However, the general tone of pictorial advertisements improved during the 1880s, and this decade also saw the appearance of a few collectors. (At this date in England enthusiasts were obliged to steal through the streets at night, removing coveted bills from their hoardings with the aid of damp sponges.) Some eminent artists now began to address themselves to the new art form. Herkomer, for instance, provided a pictorial poster for the *Magazine of Art* in 1881; and Edward Poynter an elaborate 'Minerva' design for the Guardian Fire and Life Assurance Company (1886).

Posters by academicians became more common in the late 1880s and early 1890s, but many of them were unsuited to their purpose, and it is to be regretted that the better painters generally remained aloof from this new branch of art. Discouraged by the ephemeral nature of the poster, artists were unwilling to spend time on something that would as likely as not be torn to shreds by wind and soaked by rain within a few days. And of course a stigma still attached to the activity of designing for the hoardings – especially in the minds of older artists. Even Walter Crane, whose own contributions played a modest part in the development of the pictorial advertisement in England, never quite reconciled himself to the role of posterist disliking, as he put it, 'vulgar commercial puffing'.

4 Philip Wilson Steer, poster for an exhibition at the Goupil Gallery, 1894.

5 Maurice Greiffenhagen, black-and-white version of a poster for the *Pall Mall Budget*, 1894.

6 L. Raven-Hill, poster for *Pick-Me-Up*.

NDER THE INFLUENCE OF FRENCH EXAMPLES, THE NEW 'PICTORIAL' poster became more widespread in England during the early 1890s, and between 1893 and 1894 some very talented artists turned their attention to this art form. Advertisements for exhibitions and illustrated papers were among the most important outlets for the best of the new designers, as can be seen from Philip Wilson Steer's poster for an exhibition mounted at the Goupil Gallery in 1894 [4], Maurice Greiffenhagen's *Pall Mall Budget* poster of 1894 [5], and some small bills by L. Raven-Hill for the comic journal *Pick-Me-Up* [6]. English collectors of pictorial posters increased in number during the early and mid-1890s, and dealers set up in business to supply their needs. A pictorial poster exhibition at the Westminster Aquarium, London (1894) and volumes such as Charles Hiatt's *Picture Posters* (1895) reflected a growing interest in this field.

English designers of the early 1890s were attracted, above all, to the theatre poster, and it was the theatre posters of the time that were to point the way to the future. Pre-eminent among the designers of theatre bills was Dudley Hardy, the man who is credited with having introduced the colour poster into England with his *Yellow Girl* for Jerome K. Jerome's *To-Day* magazine. Hardy was one of the first poster artists to realise that simplicity is the key to success in pictorial advertising. His saucy *Gaiety Girl* [7], which first appeared in 1893, is one of a number of bold and spirited advertisements for London theatres in which emphasis is placed on liveliness of outline rather than detail. This dashing girl in her bright red costume owes something to the work of the Frenchman Jules Chéret, whose lithographic posters had first appeared on the English hoardings in the late 1880s; and indeed one can fairly speak of Hardy's posters as the British version of Gallic *joie-de-vivre*. Hiatt (1895) remarked that the end-of-century girl whom Dudley Hardy depicted with such amazing verve and abandon was 'too light-hearted, too irresponsible, to be a daughter of this land of grey and rainy skies', but in retrospect the vivacity of the *Gaiety Girl* seems to us to represent well the spirit of 1890s London.

When, in later years, James Pryde set down some of his recollections of the English hoardings in the early 1890s, he made a particular point of mentioning the work of Greiffenhagen and Hardy. But it is clear that of all the posters he saw in London in his youth, the one he remembered most vividly was Aubrey Beardsley's advertisement for a double bill that opened at the Avenue Theatre in March 1894 [8]. This enigmatic placard, which featured a woman in a daring *décolleté* gown gazing mysteriously through a gauze curtain, was the most remarkable work of its kind yet seen in London. ('Ave a new poster', quipped *Punch*, in a punning reference to the name of the theatre.) Nothing so compelling or so irresistible, wrote Hiatt in 1895, had ever been posted in the metropolis before. 'Some gazed at it with awe, as if it were the final achievement of modern art; others jeered at it as a palpable piece of buffoonery: everybody, however, from the labourer hurrying in the dim light of morning to his work, to the prosperous stockbroker on his way to the "House", was forced to stop and look at it.'

It would be wrong to assume that the posters of Greiffenhagen, Hardy and Beardsley transformed the hoardings of the early 1890s: Pryde himself spoke of them as mere 'oases' in a desert of mediocre advertisements. But few artists could fail to notice these pioneers of the true pictorial poster; and indeed Hiatt makes it clear that the work of Hardy, Greiffenhagen and Beardsley was responsible for encouraging many 'clever young men' to take up poster designing. Foremost among these men were of course Pryde and Nicholson. It is not possible to say whether it was they who first offered to design a poster for W. S. Hardy's production of *Hamlet*; but it is certain that the two men identified the pictorial poster as a challenge a progressive modern artist could not ignore.

In responding to this challenge Pryde and Nicholson decided to work as a team. Why did they take this most unusual course? Successful collaboration is a rare thing in the visual arts, and the likelihood of two men who differed so much in their outlook and methods achieving it might seem slim. And yet, from the moment when they first met in the late 1880s Pryde and Nicholson had developed an unusual affinity. Their decision to collaborate on the *Hamlet* poster cannot be explained simply in terms of friendship or the new relationship that followed Nicholson's marriage to Pryde's sister. Nor had it much to do with the economic advantages (such as they were) of pooling their talents, although this became an important factor very shortly afterwards. The unique partnership was formed at a time when both men were finding that the stimulus of each other's ideas went some way towards compensating for the failure of conventional academic training to set them on the road to their artistic goals. It is significant that the period during which Pryde and Nicholson worked as a team lasted only two or three years: that is to say, about as long as it took the two young men to develop their individual identities as artists.

7 Dudley Hardy, poster for *A Gaiety Girl*, 1893.

HAMLET

GORDON CRAIG TOLD W. S. HARDY THAT HE KNEW A 'GREAT ARTIST' who had agreed to make some posters showing him in the role of Hamlet. Hardy fell in with the plan, and work on the project went ahead in July 1894.

Pryde and Nicholson made an arresting design (now no longer extant) in which the pictorial motif was a profile view of Hamlet holding Yorick's skull [9]. Judging by some remarks in his *Index to the story of my days* about the impact on provincial audiences of the graveyard soliloquy, the choice of motif may originally have been Craig's. The figure of the Prince of Denmark – a silhouette cut out of black paper – is composed of a flat, ungradated black that contrasts with the pale tone of the lining of the robe and the bone-white colour of the skull. The severity of the silhouette is heightened by the angularity of the outline, that of the feet and hair in particular showing the characteristic effects of scissors. Although the forms are simplified to a degree, some small-scale details (such as Hamlet's ring) are important components of the composition.

8 Aubrey Beardsley, poster for a double bill at the Avenue Theatre, London, 1894. Beardsley's work showed the Beggarstaffs that a poster's pictorial element need not be related to the subject matter of its letterpress.

9 J. & W. Beggarstaff, *Hamlet*, 1894 (design for a poster; dimensions unknown). From a reproduction in the *Magazine of Art*, January 1895.

10 J. & W. Beggarstaff, *Hamlet*, 1894 (stencil; dimensions unknown). From a reproduction in *Pan*, February 1896.

Silhouettes had already been employed in the early posters of Toulouse-Lautrec [20]; but the figure in the *Hamlet* design, which differs from French examples in its uncompromising boldness and its isolation from frame and lettering, seems to have been inspired rather by Beardsley's drawings of members of the cast of *Becket*, a Lyceum production of Henry Irving's [11]. Also influential were the shadow portraits that were popular in the era before photography. These portraits – or 'silhouettes' – were revived during the early 1890s by such artists as Nicholson's friend Phil May [18]. In the *Hamlet* poster as printed [10, **I**], where the 'cut-out' character of the outline is more marked than it is in the preliminary design, reminiscences of the old shadow portraits are quite striking.

11 Aubrey Beardsley, *Geneviève Ward as Queen Eleanor*. One of a series of drawings of players in Henry Irving's production of *Becket* at the Lyceum Theatre, London, published in the *Pall Mall Budget*, 9 February 1893.

Once the initial design for the *Hamlet* poster had been completed, stencils were made and printing could go ahead. The printing was done on ordinary brown wrapping paper. (The use of brown paper in this and other early posters was probably suggested by Pryde, who had long been using it as a half-tone ground in his pastels.) Although small details, such as Hamlet's ring, had to be hand-painted, the technique of stencil was quite adequate for an overall design in which the principal motif was a flat, black silhouette. Stencil had the additional advantage of cheapness, and the brown paper also helped to keep costs to a minimum.

Craig was later to recall seeing the printing of the poster taking place in the large double room at the Eight Bells that was used as a studio. 'Nicholson printed the thing by hand, quite amazingly,' he wrote in *Index to the story of my days*. 'He had a long table composed of four trestles and many long planks, and on this he laid a great roll of brown paper, and unrolled it as he stencilled the life-size figure of Hamlet over and over again. It was quite an achievement, but just in Nicholson's line. Pryde was usually upstairs in bed; Mrs Nicholson was preparing a "three-cornered" steak, and little Ben was toddling about, one-and-a-half years old.' These were the circumstances in which the first product of the new partnership was created.

The two versions of the published poster [10, **I**] differ in a number of respects from the preliminary design, providing evidence that the Beggarstaffs' pursuit of formal perfection did not cease once the design was completed, but continued during the process of making stencils. The introduction of a cowl in Hamlet's costume added a lively arabesque to the figure's outline, and the removal of one of the prince's feet helped to create a purer profile. The *profil perdu* to be seen in the original design was abandoned in favour of a posture that allowed the artists to depict the features of the face. Although Craig himself disliked what he termed the 'girlishness' of his own youthful features, this modification leads to greater realism and formal interest. Finally, the design in its printed form benefits from the increase in weight and compactness that was brought to the lettering of the play's title. Collectively, these changes brought a simplicity, boldness, gravity and refinement of form to the work that enables the finished product to stand comparison with a Holbein or Velázquez.

It is interesting to note that Gordon Craig regarded Nicholson as being responsible for the lion's share of the work on the *Hamlet* poster; and in a letter to Hudson dated 16 April 1948 Craig elaborated on this question – one he had already touched on in *Index to the story of my days*. The poster, he remarked, was 'done by Nicholson and presumably JP worked too – though here Nicholson was the more active of the two'. The omission of any mention of the *Hamlet* poster in the short account that Pryde wrote of the partnership lends some credibility to Craig's views on the authorship of this particular work; but it is probable that

Craig was led to overestimate the extent of Nicholson's responsibility here and elsewhere by the prominent role that the latter played during the printing stage.

Pryde and Nicholson decided that they would sign the *Hamlet* poster with a pseudonym. It is possible that they did not want their excursion into commercial art to prejudice their careers as painters in any way, but there is no concrete evidence that they wished to conceal their real identities, and they seem simply to have regarded a single pseudonym as a conveniently brief alternative to their own two names, and an appropriate symbol of the idea that their work was the product of equal endeavour. When the anonymous reporter from *The Idler* asked the artists a year or two later how they came to choose the soubriquet 'Beggarstaff', Nicholson explained that 'Pryde and I came across it one day in an old stable, on a sack of fodder. It is a good, hearty, old English name, and it appealed to us; so we adopted it immediately.'[1] Pryde's later version of how the name was discovered varies slightly from Nicholson's (Pryde believed it was he alone who had discovered the name and suggested its use), but his account is substantially the same. Initially Pryde and Nicholson signed themselves 'J. & W. Beggarstaff', and in due course this led a number of their admirers to refer to them as 'the Beggarstaff Brothers'. However, the artists themselves, although brothers-in-law, hardly ever employed this description, and Nicholson in particular protested against the use of the word brothers.

Gordon Craig recalled that he took a number of examples of the *Hamlet* poster to Hereford at the end of August 1894, a week before the play was due to be staged there. However, his employer, Hardy, was less than enthusiastic about the work. 'I don't think he was expecting what I showed him,' Craig remarked. 'Hardy's jaw dropped when he saw there was not a touch of colour in the design! He said, "But a poster's got to have colour!" Whereas Nicholson thought, like everybody else, that Hamlet was a matter of black and white . . . Anyhow, I unrolled about twenty or thirty of these marvellous posters. Hardy . . . shook his head and growled before the wonderful work of Nicholson . . . However, I believe he paid Nicholson the paltry sum he asked for the mere paper and half the time the job took; and the poster was put up and went round Hereford on a cart.' Gordon Craig's son Edward later claimed that this was done at his father's own expense.[2]

The reproduction in the February 1896 issue of *Pan* [10] shows that the figure of Hamlet in the version of the poster that was used to advertise the play was conceived in relation to plain, clearly legible lettering, and that this lettering was originally to be seen above as well as below the figure. However, although the reference above Hamlet's head to the theatre company balances the lettering below the figure, it was omitted from the limited edition of the poster that the Beggarstaffs printed at a later stage to satisfy the demands of collectors **[I]**. The omission enhanced the impact of the pictorial motif, and nothing was lost by making the poster's vertical emphasis less pronounced.

The challenge presented by pictorial posters had now begun to absorb Pryde and Nicholson, and they set about designing another bill for Hardy's touring company. In September 1894, shortly after the completion of the *Hamlet* poster, they produced an advertisement for Sheridan's *School for Scandal* showing Craig in the leading role of Charles Surface. Like the *Hamlet*, it was posted only in the provinces. Although in this case no examples of either the design or the finished work have survived, it seems likely that stencilled brown paper was once again employed as a low-cost alternative to lithography. Since the *School for Scandal* poster was never reproduced in the illustrated weeklies or the artists' journals, one cannot say much about its appearance beyond the fact that (as the art historian and critic Haldane Macfall's review in the 5 October 1895 issue of *St Paul's* magazine informs us) the colour scheme was a charming harmony of pink and grey – rococo tints entirely appropriate to an eighteenth-century comedy of manners.[3] Craig (who regarded this poster as the creation of Nicholson alone) wrote briefly in his diary on 10 October 1894 that it was an 'absolutely splendid' piece of work. Whether the artists themselves thought as highly of it one cannot say. Perhaps not, for it was the *Hamlet* that they chose to represent their work when they submitted contributions to the International Artistic Pictorial Poster Exhibition in London a month later.

BECKET

THE FACT THAT THE BEGGARSTAFFS' *HAMLET* AND *SCHOOL FOR Scandal* posters were now followed by another theatre bill shows that in the early months of their partnership Pryde and Nicholson were determined to concentrate on theatrical posters – a field in which some of the best poster designers of the early 1890s were working. It is quite possible that they may even have thought about specialising exclusively in this area. There is no doubt at all that Gordon Craig played a crucial role in stimulating the Beggarstaffs' interest in this field; and the importance of Craig for the partnership is underlined by the fact that the production for which the two young artists made their next advertisement, *Becket*, was again one in which Craig was professionally involved.

Becket, a gripping tragedy based on Tennyson's verse drama of 1884, opened at the Lyceum in London on 6 February 1893, the 55th birthday of the theatre's manager and leading actor, Henry Irving. The production was remarkable for the splendour of its scenery, the beauty of Charles Villiers Stanford's incidental music, the strength of the drama, and, above all, a memorable performance by Irving. 'Here was a new Irving, shorn of mannerisms, clear of diction and moved, it seemed, by an inspiration akin to that which had sustained the man whom he was impersonating . . . He seemed to lift a romantic poem to the level of tragedy, supplanting pagan finality with a Christian consummation, no less inexorable and tragic in its climax.'[4] The play was given a rapturous reception, performed by royal command before Queen Victoria at Windsor in March 1893 [12], and thereafter played to packed houses at the Lyceum until the season ended in late June. Craig (who played the part of the youngest Knight Templar in the production) recorded Nicholson as having seen the play twice.

12 Arthur Rackham, *A performance of 'Becket' at Windsor Castle*. Drawing published in the *Westminster Budget*, 24 March 1893.

The Beggarstaffs' original design for a poster to advertise *Becket* survives in the form of a collage in four colours on brown paper which is now in the Ellen Terry Memorial Museum **[II]**. As in the *Hamlet* poster, a pictorial motif consisting of a single figure in profile is combined with the plainest possible lettering. Following the Beggarstaffs' previous practice, the figure is a portrait; and in this case the artists' starting-point was a photograph of Irving as Becket by H. H. Hay Cameron that highlighted the actor's clear-cut ascetic features [13]. The limited number of flat, ungradated colours suggests that stencilled reproduction was considered. However, the artists must have realised that if their design was accepted at the Lyceum they would not need to print the edition themselves – they would merely be asked to provide a printer with a proof for lithographic reproduction.

13 H. H. Hay Cameron, *Henry Irving as Becket*, 1893. This photograph was shown at the first exhibition of the Photographic Salon, which took place at the Dudley Gallery, London, in the autumn of 1893.

The theatre critic, William Archer, remarked at the time of Irving's performance in *Becket* that Nature had designed the great actor for a prince of the church, and the Beggarstaffs were certainly successful in suggesting an aura of princely dignity. Their figure, which is strangely and not inappropriately reminiscent of donor portraits on the wings of late medieval altarpieces,[5] was possibly meant to allude to the scene in Canterbury Cathedral at the end of the play in which Becket faces his assassins, alone and defiant. Although perhaps less interesting from the formal point of view than the Beggarstaffs' profile of Hamlet, the image of Becket is a more powerful one. The American artist Joseph Pennell, merciless critic of mediocrity in poster design, called the work 'majestic'. The effect derives partly from the dramatic juxtaposition of light and dark in Becket's Augustinian habit, and partly from the monumentality of the figure. It is clear that the Beggarstaffs felt Irving's spell-binding presence could best be suggested by making the mitre enhance the impression of a man of great stature. Following the example of a representation of Irving as Becket by Beardsley,[6] the lettering of the play's title was placed to one side, thus allowing the top of the mitre to 'crown' the archbishop's head.

One of the differences between this work and the *Hamlet* is to be seen in the foreshortening of Becket's left arm: an illusionistic device that is out of keeping with the planar character of most Beggarstaff designs, and one which was avoided in later works. Another point of difference with the *Hamlet* poster is to be found in the geometric formalism of the design. This new feature, seen here in the cultivation of straight lines and semi-circular shapes, was to become more marked in subsequent designs. Something of the way in which the Beggarstaffs subjected their designs to a process of gradual refinement can be seen in the removal of the hand that Becket presses against his chest – an extraneous detail that served no useful pictorial purpose – from the version of the design which is reproduced in the September 1895 issue of *The Studio* [14]. No doubt other changes would have been made had the design been taken to the printing stage, and the most important of these might well have been the addition of the word 'Lyceum'.

The *Becket* design cannot have been made by Pryde and Nicholson before the opening of the play on 6 February 1893; and indeed the stylistic similarity of the work to the *Hamlet* bill suggests a date in the second half of 1894 – possibly about the time of the visits that Nicholson made to the Lyceum on 18 and 20 July of that year. This conclusion accords with the remark made by the art critic, Arthur Fish, in 1895, that the design was produced when *Becket* had nearly run its course. Fish claimed that the work was done as an experiment, and this seems to be a distinct possibility. Experiment or not, the design was shown to Irving. Ellen Terry, who played the part of Rosamund in the production, clearly thought that it

14 J. & W. Beggarstaff, *Becket*, 1894 (design for a poster; dimensions unknown). From a reproduction in *The Studio*, September 1895.

14

was worth using as an advertisement, but Irving was less impressed. Miss Terry recorded that the great actor-manager 'could not (for some reason unknown to any of us) see his way to publish it'.[7]

Ellen Terry, a constant source of encouragement and practical help to the Beggarstaffs, found Irving's lack of interest inexplicable. However, there are a number of possible reasons for the latter's rejection of their design. First, it was not Irving's practice to commission pictorial posters (he tended to rely mainly on letterpress advertisements in the daily and weekly newspapers); and of course there was little need to depart from this routine to advertise a drama which had already been playing to crowded and enthusiastic houses for over a year. If the actor *had* seen the need for a pictorial poster, he would probably have invited Seymour Lucas, Alma Tadema, Ford Madox Brown, Hawes Craven or one of the other artists who worked for him on scenery and costumes to submit ideas. Second, it is difficult to imagine the Beggarstaffs' austere design appealing to a man with Irving's limited capacity for the appreciation of art. Finally, Irving was inclined to be very critical of the images of himself that artists created, particularly where they showed him in a play that held a special place in his affections, as *Becket* did. So hard to please was he that on one occasion he turned down a portrait of himself by Whistler which the artist offered to him for only £7. He was especially concerned that the images which were handed on to posterity matched the images he himself was attempting to communicate to his audiences; and if an artist fell short of his requirements in this respect he could be ruthless. H. A. Jones told how Irving, displeased with Sargent's portrait of him, bought the painting and cut it to pieces.[8] In the circumstances, it is remarkable that the Beggarstaffs should have had the audacity to submit their *Becket* design to Irving at all.

The Beggarstaffs at Work

HOW DID THE PRODUCTS OF THIS NEWLY FORMED PARTNERSHIP take shape? 'One of us gets an idea,' explained Pryde. 'We talk it over, the other suggests an addition, the matter is considered, perhaps shelved away for months.[9] Finally we draw the design very roughly with charcoal, on big sheets of paper, and then place the lines and masses in their places on the groundwork, which is generally of ordinary brown paper.' Shapes representing the masses were then cut out of coloured paper and placed against the background. Next, 'we walked round and had a look at it,' said Nicholson, 't'see whether we'd alter the colours'. Alterations to the colours, shapes and positions of the cut-outs were invariably necessary, and after these had been made the pieces of coloured paper were pasted down, as in the *Becket* design now at the Ellen Terry Museum. A comment made by Hiatt (1895) about a design called *Nobody's Pianos* suggests that the Beggarstaffs used a brush from time to time, but paint was generally confined to lettering and intricate details. In the case of speculative designs (those not linked to a specific product) the lettering was left to a later stage.

In a remark published in *Postscript to Image*, Nicholson pointed out how much easier it was to work with coloured paper than paints when producing designs; and he also hinted at the advantages of the procedure to artists who were conscious of the importance of outline. Pryde, too, in the autobiographical essay he wrote towards the end of his life, noted that the 'flat effect' created by this method was not only pictorially striking; it was also economical when it came to printing. 'Tom Browne, the black-and-white artist,' wrote Pryde, 'told me of his delight in finding that the method was so easy to reproduce.'

The slow pace at which Pryde proceeded (his creative method was characterised by short bursts of frenzied activity interspersed with long intervals of cogitation), combined with the artists' endless revision of their work, meant that individual Beggarstaff designs were usually a long time in reaching completion. The art critic, J. A. Reid, was told by Nicholson in 1900 that the two artists spent weeks conceiving and working out their ideas, and the correspondent from *The Idler* who interviewed the Beggarstaffs during the winter of 1895–6 reported that it was common for the two artists to work well into the night. The Beggarstaffs would occasionally produce more than one design when working on a poster (at least three were made during work on the *Don Quixote*), and then the length of time spent on a project would be greater still. The amount of labour that the Beggarstaffs put into their designs was, however, never obvious in the final product. This irritated Pryde, who complained that 'people are rather prone to imagine that, because a thing looks easy when finished, it must have been easy to do'.

When the journalist, Ranger Gull, visited the Beggarstaffs' studio early in 1897, he noticed that the walls were lined with posters in various stages of completion. The fact that the artists always had several projects in hand did nothing to help them increase their productivity, but the option to be able to turn from one design to another was an absolutely essential part of the creative process. Pryde, in particular, believed in the importance of the 'fresh eye'.

Once the Beggarstaffs were reasonably satisfied with a design they would seek an opinion on it from one or more fellow artists whose judgment they trusted. For instance, they would sometimes take examples of their work to show Joseph Pennell at his London house in Buckingham Gate [15].[10] Many of the designs the two artists made were speculative; others were done for specific advertisers. (The *Cinderella* and *Rowntree's Cocoa* designs that the Beggarstaffs made at the suggestion of the Artistic Supply Company are examples of the latter.) If a completed design was earmarked for immediate commercial use, a stencil or stencils would be made by the artists, further refinements on the completed design often being introduced at this point. The earlier Beggarstaff posters were hand-printed from a stencil. Later ones were reproduced by a lithographic printer from a single stencil-printed original. Although Nicholson, for one, had experience of lithography, the Beggarstaffs do not seem to have drawn any designs for posters directly on to stone. A separate edition would sometimes be printed for collectors – occasionally

15 Aubrey Beardsley, *Joseph Pennell as 'The Devil of Notre Dame'*. A caricature published in the *Pall Mall Budget* which alludes to Pennell's *Stryge* etching of 1893. Pryde and Nicholson must have met Beardsley at the gatherings of artists and writers that took place at the Pennells' London flat on Thursday evenings.

without lettering or, as in the case of *The Hour* [26b], accompanying letterpress. In some instances, the artists retained the right to exhibit and sell their original artwork after publication of a poster.

The Beggarstaffs needed a large communal studio for their work. The double room at the Eight Bells, Denham, was adequate for the production of the earliest posters, which were not very big. It was spacious enough to house the trestles that Gordon Craig described Nicholson as using during the stencilling of the *Hamlet* poster, and the 'huge collection of finished and unfinished designs' (most of them rolled up) that was mentioned by the correspondent from *The Idler*. However, when the Beggarstaffs started work on a larger scale, as they did very early on (some of the designs sent to the first International Artistic Pictorial Poster Exhibition in the autumn of 1894 were 12 feet high), they found that they needed more room, and it must have been a relief to exchange their Denham studio for the large, well-lit hall in Logan Place, Kensington, that they used after the Nicholson family's move to London. The new premises allowed the Beggarstaffs to work on the monumental scale that posters such as the large version of *Rowntree's Elect Cocoa* involved. Ranger Gull, who visited the artists in their new studio, noted that instead of easels the hall contained a huge table and some immense stepladders. Gull asked the Beggarstaffs to illustrate the 'difficulties and dangers incidental to the making of a poster', and he could readily appreciate, after seeing the two artists perched in curious attitudes on top of their ladders, that (as Nicholson said) 'to do posters you must be an acrobat as well as an artist'.

The Beggarstaffs were reluctant to let people think that their respective contributions to the posters they designed were anything but equal; and if contemporaries of the two men sometimes received the misleading impression that Nicholson brought more to the partnership than Pryde it was simply because Pryde never allowed anyone to see him at work, while Nicholson positively enjoyed the presence of an audience. The artists themselves would not allow that either one of them played a greater part than the other in the creation of their posters. Neither man, remarked the anonymous journalist from *The Idler*, would confess to having a greater power of imagination than the other, nor to possessing any quality, in a marked degree, which in the other was not equally noticeable.

On the question of whether the nature of their respective contributions could be distinguished, the Beggarstaffs were just as adamant. As the *Idler* journalist remarked, 'their methods seem to be so dovetailed in from the conception of an idea to its final expression, that we could learn nothing more exact as to their differences of feeling, than that Pryde generally uses a penknife to cut out the masses of coloured paper which form their original designs, while Nicholson employs a pair of scissors. Living intimately together in the same house for some years, and working daily together on the same pictures, they are in such thorough accord that, an idea once started, it seems to travel backwards and forwards, from one brain to the other, gradually picking up its character, until it reaches its final and perfect form.' The impression given by this description is of an exceptionally harmonious working relationship; and indeed there is no reason why this should not have been the true state of affairs: the two men were close friends at this stage in their lives, and Nicholson had already developed a capacity for friendly collaboration even before he began his partnership with Pryde.[11]

It is quite possible, however, that the respective roles of the two artists did, in practice, differ fundamentally, with Pryde, who was curiously clumsy when it came to doing anything with his hands, making his most important contribution

16 James Pryde, cover for the February 1899 issue of *The Poster*. The publication in this issue of Hiatt's important article on Pryde and Nicholson coincided with the brief revival of the Beggarstaff partnership that occurred at the time of the *Robespierre* project.

1899
February
The Poster
Pryde
Number VIII
Volume II
Price Sixpence net

16

The World of Dress
Edited by Mrs Aria.
Spring Number
Price 1/.
C.H.S.
William Nicholson 1899.
Fashions of London, Paris, Vienna and New York
Vol. II. No. 14.]
CONTENTS.
[MAY, 1899.
Beautiful Women in Beautiful Gowns. The Marchioness of Londonderry.
Modes of the Month in London. By Mrs. Aria.
Dress on the Stage. A Chat with Miss Evelyn Millard.
Parisian Fashions.
Dress in New York.
"A Fitting Retaliation." A Dialogue. By Mrs. Barry Pain.
The Talk of Society.
Dress in Vienna.
At the Punchestown Races.
Theatrical Dress in London. (At the Lyceum, the Criterion, Her Majesty's, and the Adelphi.)
Famous Lace (Illustrated with Specimens), in the possession of Lady Brougham.
Fashionable Millinery.
The Newest Jewellery.
Selected Models from Selected Establishments in London.
Result of Dress Competition. Prizes: 5 guineas; 3 guineas; 2 guineas.
"A Couple of Cowards." A Short Story by Effie Adelaide Rowlands.
Notes on Needlework.
Our Own Fireside.
&c., &c.

17

at the time when ideas for designs were first conceived, and Nicholson, who was incredibly dexterous, assuming a leading role when it came to the execution of those ideas.[12] Pryde's reliance on Nicholson when it came to the technical aspects of poster-making is confirmed by Craig's description of the younger artist working alone on the printing of the *Hamlet* bill. So far as the formal qualities of the Beggarstaffs' posters are concerned, it seems – to judge from the works that the two men produced as individuals – that Nicholson brought a certain boldness and breadth to the treatment of masses, while Pryde brought graphic invention. But while comparisons of the work of Pryde and Nicholson [16, 17] occasionally provide insights into their respective contributions to the partnership, they are not always as revealing as one might expect, underlining the degree to which the Beggarstaffs succeeded in merging their separate personalities and talents in their posters.

The Westminster Aquarium Exhibition of 1894

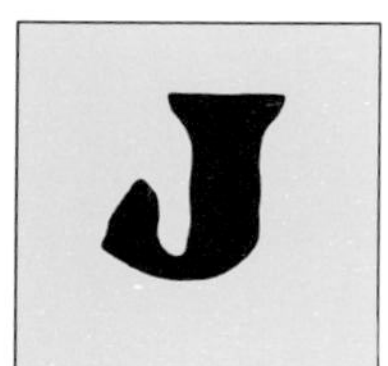

James Pryde claimed that the Beggarstaffs' reasons for taking up poster designing were purely financial. He and his partner were both feeling the pinch, which was perhaps particularly worrying for Nicholson with his young family. Steen recorded that the latter had been promised an allowance of £150 per annum by his father after his marriage; but this arrangement was discontinued after a short time owing to a temporary difficulty at 'the works', and the artist was forced to support his wife and child by his own efforts alone.

'We are both intensely fond of painting,' Pryde remarked to the anonymous journalist from *The Idler*, 'but one cannot always sell one's pictures.' The two men considered trying their hands at pen drawings for the illustrated papers, but came to the conclusion that they could not work in what they called the 'conventional style' that publishers demanded. Fortunately, there was an alternative: as Pryde pointed out, poster work was at that time proving 'remunerative', and so, 'seeing very great chances of it in England, we decided to adopt that'. Arthur Fish tells the same story: in the September 1895 issue of *The Studio* he reported that J. & W. Beggarstaff took up poster-making as the only way in which they could afford the luxury of painting pictures. It was a step that many other aspiring painters took at this time; indeed some young artists even abandoned their studies in Paris when the poster boom raised the prospect of a prosperous career in commercial design. So, while the Beggarstaffs saw the *Hamlet* commission as an artistic challenge rather than a means of earning money, it was not long before hopes of financial remuneration became their principal reason for designing posters. Exactly when Pryde and Nicholson took the decision to become professional

17 William Nicholson, cover for the spring number of *The World of Dress*, 1899.

18 Phil May, *Official at the Westminster Aquarium*, 1890. The economy of May's black-and-white drawings was much admired by Pryde and Nicholson. May himself was a close friend and source of practical help to the two poster designers.

19 Jules Chéret, black-and-white version of a poster for the *Folies Bergères*, 1893. The central feature of the first Aquarium exhibition was a huge panel devoted to the work of Chéret and Lautrec.

designers is not known, but it must have been before an exhibition of 'pictorial posters' was opened in London in the autumn of 1894.

The International Artistic Pictorial Poster Exhibition opened at the Westminster (or 'Royal') Aquarium, London, on 23 October 1894, promoted by an entrepreneur named Edward Bella. In addition to printing posters, Bella acted as an agent for commercial firms who were looking for designs. He was also active as an art dealer. He is remembered today chiefly as a patron of Toulouse-Lautrec (from whom he commissioned an advertisement for confetti), but his real importance lies mainly in the two exhibitions that he organised at the Westminster Aquarium as a means of stimulating public interest in the posters he supplied to collectors.

The old Westminster Aquarium, now demolished (the original site is covered by the Central Hall), was built in the 1870s in emulation of the Brighton Aquarium. As an establishment that aspired to educate the public, it was a failure from the start; and soon after its opening sword swallowers, contortionists, two-headed nightingales and other monstrosities were introduced to augment the waning attractions of the fish. In the late 1870s and early 1880s the Aquarium was one of the sights of the capital and, when the young William Nicholson arrived in London in 1880 on his father's election as member of parliament for Newark, the renowned palace of varieties was one of the first places he visited. Little did he know at that time that it would be there, alongside the singing donkeys, Matabele warriors and live ostriches, that his work would first attract critical notice. It was not Burlington House, but then the poster was still some way from being regarded as an art form worthy of serious consideration [18].

Nicholson visited Bella's International Artistic Pictorial Poster Exhibition with Gordon Craig shortly before it was officially opened to the public. Other artists were there, including Toulouse-Lautrec, who was in charge of the French section. Nearly 200 posters and a number of designs for posters were displayed in the open galleries of the building, where they created a blaze of colour above the heads of visitors who had come to see the boxing kangaroo, Zulima the female Samson and other attractions in the hall below. Nothing of the kind had ever been seen in England before. The exhibits were, without exception, 'artistic' posters (as distinct from ordinary commercial work), and many of them were theatre bills. On show were English posters by, among others, Frank Brangwyn, Beardsley, Crane, Greiffenhagen, Hardy, Raven-Hill and Steer. However, the majority of the exhibits were from France, with many contributions from Grasset, Willette, Chéret [19], Lautrec [20] and Steinlen [21]. The many vivacious posters by Jules Chéret undoubtedly made the biggest impact, but a dozen striking works by Lautrec also caught the eye. Craig was particularly impressed by the seductive young lady in Pierre Bonnard's 'wonderful' advertisement for the *Revue Blanche* [22].

Pryde and Nicholson had submitted five works to the exhibition: an example of their *Hamlet* poster and four unpublished designs. The latter are described by Pryde in his autobiographical essay as 'not for any particular firm's commodity but merely for a given article to which the firm's name [i.e., the firm buying the design] could be applied . . . We made them fairly large, for some were twelve feet high.' Pryde said that these four designs were made specially for the exhibition; that they involved silhouettes; and that they were made by cutting shapes out of coloured paper and then pasting these cut-outs on to flat boards or paper.

Contemporary descriptions record a few details of the appearance of the Beggarstaffs' four speculative designs. The design in two colours entitled *Nobody's Washing Blue* depicted a black figure separated from a black background by a fine white contour, the only colour being a very large blue blot in a wash basin. (Spielmann referred to the effect in this design of 'fine white lines and blue spots upon a black ground'.) The descriptions of this work suggest that here the Beggarstaffs had Beardsley's celebrated *Comedy of Sighs* bill at the back of their minds.

In a four-colour collage for *Nobody's Candles* a girl holding a lighted candle stood boldly out in black against a yellow background. The candle threw a heavy black shadow against this background, and the girl 'melted into' this shadow in a marvellous way. Joseph Pennell regarded this as the finest of the designs that the Beggarstaffs submitted to the Aquarium exhibition.[13]

The Beggarstaffs' design in four colours for *Nobody's Niggers* appears to have been intended as an advertisement for a negro minstrel show. Unfortunately, no description at all of this particular work can be traced.

The artists' fourth design, also in four colours, was entitled *Nobody's Pianos*. This bold design showed, in the foreground, a long-haired musician seated at a large black grand piano. The setting was a concert hall, and a listening audience was represented, behind the pianist, receding row by row into the distance. Pennell remarked on the '*supercherie spirituelle*' with which the audience as well as the piano was represented. Haldane Macfall (1895/1), who described this effort as 'delightfully funny as well as being capital in design and good taste', commented on the boldness of the design; but added that it could not be compared to the Beggarstaffs' later work. Macfall's judgment was echoed by the Beggarstaffs themselves in a reference they made to all four 'Nobody' designs a few years later, for Hiatt reported in 1899 that the artists refused him permission to reproduce these designs on the grounds that they were 'early works of insufficient merit'.

A reviewer in the 27 October 1894 issue of the *Athenaeum* warned his readers that he could only recommend Bella's exhibition to 'those who, provided it is done in a new way, have no objection to being offended as well as amused'. This sour note was not, however, typical, and most critics agreed with Spielmann, who wrote in the 3 November 1894 issue of *The Graphic* that the exhibition had a serious purpose and was an important milestone in a new branch of art. 'The exhibition of artistic "posters" now being held at the Royal Aquarium,' he said, 'should be visited by everybody in the remotest degree interested in public advertising or in the beautifying of the streets. Vast improvement has within recent years been made in England in the art of poster designing; but the present show will teach visitors how colour and style may be imparted, and how commercial needs may be bent to the highest artistic beauty.' In a postscript to his remarks on the importance of the exhibition in general, Spielmann observed that one effect of the exhibition would be 'the making of certain English reputations which have hitherto been unnoticed – at least in London'.

The show certainly made the Beggarstaffs' reputation. Many critics admired the 'Nobody' designs (Fish claimed that they were almost unanimous in their praise of these works), but it was the *Hamlet* that impressed people most. Some years later, Frank Rutter wrote that 'though the French posters attracted a great deal of attention, the great sensation of the show was an English exhibit, a *Hamlet*, stencilled in four colours, catalogued as being the work of "Beggarstaff Brothers". Later it leaked out that this was the trading name of two young artists,

20 Henri de Toulouse-Lautrec, poster for the *Moulin Rouge*, 1891. Nicholson saw La Goulue dancing with Valentin le Désossé at the Moulin Rouge when he was a student in Paris in 1889–90.

21 Théophile Steinlen's image from 1894 of a young girl drinking milk was used in France on a poster for *Lait pur de la Vingeanne Stérilisé* and in England for *Nestlé's Swiss Milk*.

22 Pierre Bonnard poster for *La Revue Blanche*, 1894.

William Nicholson and James Pryde. At a time when the nearest approach to art to be seen on the London hoardings was Millais' *Bubbles*, it may be imagined what a commotion was caused by the Beggarstaff *Hamlet*, an austerely grand design with no details, no bright colours and – worst of all – no pretty faces. It was staggering in its simplicity. But even those who did not like it, could not forget it and found themselves talking about it.'

The conjunction of French and English works in the exhibition encouraged comparisons of exhibits from opposite sides of the Channel; and a number of references were made to the way in which the Beggarstaffs had disdained French *joie-de-vivre*. One critic, Spielmann, remarked that the Beggarstaffs' 'gloomy' contributions were 'about as like to Chéret's posy-like *affiches* as a grim and ascetic old Carmelite is like to a lady of the *corps de ballet*'.[14] It was of course true; but fair-minded critics could point out that the Beggarstaffs had rejected not only the frivolity of Chéret, but also what was seen at the time as the 'grotesque' aspects of Lautrec's work. They had, in short, adopted a discriminating attitude to French art: a judicious, selective approach that reflected their native good sense.

The so-called 'Englishness' of the Beggarstaffs' work was, in fact, frequently commented on by visitors to the Aquarium exhibition. 'Knowing ones,' commented Rutter, 'professed to perceive a parallel in the work of Toulouse-Lautrec, and chattered about Pryde and Nicholson having studied in Paris: but to most of us their work seemed then, as it does still, to be essentially English'. Macfall, writing in the 26 June 1895 issue of *St Paul's*, stressed the Englishness of the Beggarstaffs by contrasting their work with the 'refined, perfumed, and even perverse' productions of Beardsley and other representatives of the 'Decadents'. It was shortly after the arrest of Oscar Wilde, and Macfall was attacking the idea that Wilde and Beardsley were 'types' of late Victorian art. To Macfall – an ex-army officer given to the forthright expression of fairly conservative views – the work of Beardsley was effeminate, sexless and unclean. It was not English at all, but utterly 'foreign'. The robust and healthy work of Pryde and Nicholson was, by contrast, English through and through. This was to be the platform for the friendly reception which many other critics gave the Beggarstaffs in the aftermath of the Wilde affair.

THE NEW ART OF ADVERTISING

THE RESTRICTION OF THE WESTMINSTER AQUARIUM EXHIBITS TO work produced in France and England drew attention to the extent to which the English lagged behind the French in the 'artistic' quality of their posters.

There were many reasons for the artistic superiority of French advertisements in the early 1890s. In France, the custom of using pictorial posters to advertise illustrated books and periodicals had been established for some time; music-halls and cabarets (important patrons of the artistic poster) were numerous; and colour lithography was more advanced. Above all, the French actually believed in the value of commissioning designs from good artists. Joseph Thacher Clarke, writing in the catalogue of the 1894 Aquarium exhibition, noted that while the 'commercial' poster still existed in France, most astute French advertising agents – looking at the matter solely from a business point of view – found that really artistic work actually paid better in cash results.

In England, pictorial posters had long been of a very low standard; and relatively little had changed by 1892, when the English poster was 'still outside the current of decorative endeavours which has given us the Morris wallpapers, the Doulton tiles, the Walter Crane book-covers, and the Cobden Sanderson bindings'.[15] A major obstacle to change was the advertising profession, which was not yet convinced of the effectiveness of artistic designs. Moreover, the rent of hoardings was often very high in England, and advertisers were unwilling to spend an additional large sum – which could be anything from £20 to £100 – on an artistic design that might well then cost more to reproduce than the design itself.

When the first International Artistic Pictorial Poster Exhibition opened in London in 1894, the question of the value of artistic posters became the subject of intense debate. Were artistic posters more likely to attract the attention of the man in the street than posters which were not artistic? Were they more effective in persuading people to buy the product advertised? The public, more concerned about the proliferation in towns and cities of large numbers of unsightly advertisements, joined in the debate.

Writing in the January 1895 issue of the *Windsor Magazine*, Gleeson White, editor of *The Studio*, remarked on the widespread interest in 'artistic' posters that the Westminster Aquarium exhibition had aroused. 'How far has the new craze of the moment spread?' he asked. 'Beginning in Paris, it attacked America years ago, and now descends in force upon London. That Art, which has always protested against the desecration of our streets by hoardings covered with placards, should suddenly resolve to mend and not end them, should patronise the poster, and bestow upon it the latest eccentricities by the most "advanced" decorators, is even less wonderful than that folks should collect them. Yet the movement is already well established. Collectors of repute, learned fellows of societies, are turning from prints and pottery, carvings and coins, to the illustrated poster. At present, indeed, they are drawing the line at genuinely artistic specimens, but the craze once started may soon throw aside any trammels, and then all the horrors of the hoarding will be hunted for and carefully mounted, catalogued, described, and sold at high prices . . .

Crazes and hobbies enough and to spare,
Our forbears have left us. Now, say, is it right
For leaders of taste a new cult to declare,
Exploiting new hobbies our greed to excite?
Postage stamps, book-plates, blue china and quite
Dozens of things most aesthetic and mystic,
Pass for the moment away out of sight –
Now is the cult of the poster artistic' [23]

23 Advertisement from the 1890s for the London branch of a dealer in artistic posters. Firms such as Huardel supplied collectors with decorative panels and designs for posters as well as printed work. They also acted as agents for advertisers who were looking for ideas.

Although Gleeson White's remarks apply principally to collectors, it was because some English businessmen were now beginning to admit that the French might be right about the effectiveness of the 'artistic' poster – and so were patronising the poster artists – that there were posters to collect. The question these advertisers were now asking themselves was: what kind of artistic design was best suited to their commercial purpose? In attempting to find solutions to this problem, the efforts of the advertisers and their agents had, of course, long been misdirected. Brander Matthews pointed to the celebrated case of Pears, the soapmakers, who 'plastered up all over London, in a printed gilt frame, an elaborate chromo-lithographic facsimile of an oil painting by Sir John Millais, of which the merits, such as they are, are purely pictorial, and in no wise decorative'. The graphic style of artists such as Linley Sambourne and Walter Crane had not been very much more appropriate; and by 1894 manufacturers began to realise that it was not enough to commission a sketch from a *Punch* artist or purchase the copyright of a painting by an eminent academician. It was necessary to get an artist who understood the principles of pictorial advertising to work specifically for the hoardings.

The Aquarium exhibition showed that by the early 1890s several English artists had recognised that the ideal pictorial poster was a mural decoration with its own conventions and limitations, and a few advertisers were prepared to support them by buying their designs. A notice in the 10 November 1894 issue of *Black and White* documents this turning point in the history of the English placard. 'It seems strange that London, the richest, and, in matters of commercial advertising, the most speculative city in Europe, should so lag behind Paris in this question of street bills. The truth is, it was not want of funds or enterprise that has kept us back – it was our gross stupidity and ineptitude to understand the demands of the new conditions . . . Now and then an artist half seized the real idea. This you can see in the Aquarium today . . . But though the Dudley Hardys, the Greiffenhagens, Raven Hills, and Phil Mays of today may be only imitators of Chéret, Lautrec and Company at present, they are distinctly beginning to understand the new laws of the new art, and ultimately must develop a native school. They have no false pride; they work direct for the hoardings. This is already much.'

What were these new laws of the new art to which *Black and White* refers? Although advertisers were less daunted by the costs of colour lithography by the end of the nineteenth century, designs which could be reproduced cheaply were preferred. As far as function was concerned, the posters of the 1890s had to stand out from the advertisements that surrounded them on the hoardings; they had to be capable of arresting the attention of a passer-by (who might be travelling along on the top of a horse-bus, some distance away); they had to detain the attention of the passer-by for long enough to communicate their message; and they had to imprint themselves, if possible, on the spectator's memory. The reviewer of the Aquarium exhibition in the 15 December 1894 issue of the *Saturday Review* reveals that the general consensus of opinion among those who had begun to think about the matter was that English artists who sought to meet these requirements should adopt the 'brilliant but simple effect of colour, and the breadth of . . . masses' to be found in the best French advertisements.

Hardy, Greiffenhagen, Raven Hill and others had already put the new principles to use in advertisements that successfully fulfilled their commercial purpose; and the Beggarstaffs now showed at the Aquarium that they, too, understood that breadth and simplicity were prerequisites of the modern pictorial poster. As Macfall (1895/2) pointed out, 'the use of simple means for advertisement, that is, the necessity for decorative means, such as large eloquent silhouettes, and of broad sweeps and patches of colour, and of expressive line, has been fully understood by the young artists'. At this stage, nobody doubted that the Beggarstaffs' work was anything but the perfect vehicle for effective advertising. As Hiatt (1895) said, the designs of Pryde and Nicholson 'are at once striking and artistic. They cry their wares well, and they are a delight to the eye'.

Posters on Approval

HIATT WAS AMONG THE CRITICS WHO PROPHESIED A BRIGHT future for the Beggarstaffs, and wrote in *Picture Posters*: 'If "Nobody" is not rapidly converted into "somebody", the various manufacturers and proprietors of the articles mentioned . . . must be very stupid people.' The two young artists, encouraged by the prospect of success, took to what Pryde described as 'doing posters for actual firms on approval' – a job which involved taking samples of their work to the advertising managers of selected companies. Phil May made a drawing of Pryde and Nicholson hawking their designs round London in this way, enormous rolls of paper under their arms. A revised version of this drawing (the rolls of paper omitted) was later published in *The Studio* [24].

The driving force behind the Beggarstaffs' enterprising approach to the business of selling their work must have been the practical and hard-working Nicholson. Gordon Craig confirmed that the two artists differed fundamentally when it came to the desire and ability to capitalise on their talents. 'I knew J.P. and W.N.P.N. (whom we called "the Kid") when they were inseparable,' he wrote, '– always together in life and in work – J.P. without the faintest notion (or shall we say *wish* to learn) about business – or what it mattered – and N. quite practical, adroit, and damned if he'd become an unknown artist while Beardsley, Conder, Max B. and a whole Yellow Book of Artists had become celebrated in a night. And thanks to his practicality J.P. lived, ate, drank (and didn't gamble) and developed a worth-while personality. One can *not* forget or make little of this fact – Pryde really might have died but for Nicholson.'[16]

The young artists were not always received with open arms by advertising managers. 'Some of them expressed their unfavourable opinions with extreme frankness,' Nicholson remembered. 'One gentleman, an editor, on whom we called one day, just after he had lunched somewhat heartily, kindly went into details with us, and proceeded to measure from point to point on one of our designs with a yard rule, criticising freely as he went about his work. He warmed to his task, and his

spirit chortled within him as he gaily and innocently pointed out the innumerable defects of our designs; that is to say, all the things in which they differed from other posters.' There is a hint in Hiatt's 1899 article that the Beggarstaffs were sometimes asked by prospective clients to make changes to their designs, and it is to their credit that they never agreed to compromise. Hiatt reported: 'They will give the advertiser the best that it is in their power to give, but they will be no more induced to modify their designs to suit the supposed taste of the public than Whistler would be induced to alter his etchings of London to oblige a house agent'.

Pryde and Nicholson clearly had their disappointments, but there were successes as well. The first of these was an advertisement for Kassama Corn Flour **[III]** – a commission which may well have followed directly from the Aquarium exhibition, for it was designed, according to Hiatt (1899), in October 1894. Nothing in the image itself links this small poster exclusively with the commodity advertised, and so the work may have started life as a speculative design in which the girl's shopping basket could have accommodated any one of a wide variety of groceries. The placing of the lettering seems to have been dictated to some extent by the availability of space, and this provides some support for the conclusion that the original design may have been created without any particular product in mind. This was the first Beggarstaff poster to be published in the form of a lithograph.

The girl in the *Kassama Corn Flour* poster offers a strong contrast to the winsome, smiling maidens ('*Oh Mama, don't forget to order . . .*') encountered in other advertisements for household goods from the period. Depersonalised and distant, she imparts no information and communicates no advice. The girl's silhouette is reminiscent of the *Hamlet*, and the Beggarstaffs can hardly be criticised for repeating a formula which had brought them such success. The simplicity of the conception is again conditioned by the exigencies of the stencil technique, the girl being drawn in such a way as to allow hair and basket to print the same colour as the background. (The tiny touch of scarlet on the lips would have been hand-coloured in the original stencil.) But now the artists were giving more thought to the question of visibility; and to make the girl in the *Kassama* poster more eye-catching, they placed her silhouette against a bright yellow rather than a brown background. By surrounding the figure with a wide expanse of unrelieved yellow, they ensured that it would be isolated from adjacent advertisements. (The telling combination of black and yellow in this work may have been inspired by Beardsley's covers for the notorious *Yellow Book*, which began publication earlier in 1894.)

The Beggarstaffs rejected any suggestion that they might introduce a representation of cornflour, and only the lettering tells the viewer what is being advertised. As in earlier works, this lettering remains uniform in size and style throughout. The artists' use of scissors in the creation of the words 'Kassama Corn Flour' allowed them to relate words and pictorial component more satisfactorily than in the *Hamlet* and *Becket*. Such careful relation of lettering to image was to be characteristic of almost all the Beggarstaffs' future posters.

Not long after the Westminster Aquarium exhibition, the Beggarstaffs created a design based on the motif of a Chinaman. This design, later incorporated in an advertisement for the *A Trip to Chinatown* musical comedy [25], was a simple silhouette once again, but in this instance an asymmetrically placed one, consisting of a combination of light and dark tones against a middle-toned orange. The use of scissors is more obvious in the outline of the Chinaman figure than it is in the figures in the *Hamlet* and *Becket* posters; but an effect of recession has been introduced in the man's legs, and so the image is not a true profile. The rectangle

24 Phil May, *The Beggarstaffs*, 1895. Drawing published in *The Studio*, September 1895, and *St Paul's*, 5 October 1895. Pryde and Nicholson affected the old-fashioned high collar. The wide-spreading covert coats with big pearl buttons follow a style favoured by Phil May.

in the upper right corner of the design appears to have been incorporated for purely formal reasons. The proportions of this rectangle (four to three) were echoed by the design as a whole as it existed at the time of its adaptation in the *Trip to Chinatown* poster. The Beggarstaffs' later revision **[IV]** of the original design shows that, unlike their earlier works, the ability of the *Chinaman* design to catch the attention of passers-by depends as much on colour as on tonal contrasts.

Pryde and Nicholson may have had Japanese prints in mind when making their *Chinaman* design. White pointed out in the 1890s that designers of posters could learn from the simplicity of large masses, brilliant tints and absence of background in Japanese colour woodcuts, and indeed a number of English artists (such as Hardy and Beardsley) followed the example of the French in studying such works. The influence of Japanese prints on the Beggarstaffs can be seen mainly in the pure, flat colours of the *Chinaman* design. The rectangular panel in the upper right corner recalls similar panels in Japanese woodcuts, but generally the Beggarstaffs assimilated their experience of the formal aspects of oriental art, and borrowed motifs of this kind are rare in their work.

The *Chinaman* is almost certainly another example of a speculative design which in its original form (i.e., without any added lettering) was not tied down to any specific product; and this seems to be confirmed by Nicholson's own reference to the work as simply the 'design of a Chinaman'. As we have seen, the design was purchased to serve as an advertisement for a popular musical comedy (or 'variety play') by Charles Hoyte entitled *A Trip to Chinatown*, which opened at Toole's Theatre in London on 29 September 1894. According to William Archer, this production was 'simply a music-hall entertainment, and not a bad one as such things go. It seemed to delight the audience at Toole's Theatre on the night when I saw it, and I should not be surprised if it became very popular. The leading part is played by Mr R. G. Knowles, a stolid American "artiste", with a stentorian voice and an undeniable quaintness of style. The topics of his humour are somewhat monotonous and not over refined, but the audience does not in the least mind that'.[17] This none too serious entertainment transferred to the Strand Theatre on 17 December 1894, and it was perhaps at this point that the Beggarstaffs' design (described by the artists as 'one of our earliest things') was sold. The Chinaman motif linked tenuously with the title of the show; but it was not otherwise appropriate, for the production contained no oriental characters of any kind. However, accuracy had never been an indispensable feature of pictorial advertisements for the popular theatre: it was still common at this date for printing firms to issue 'stock' posters designed to fit many productions – placards on which the titles of the plays they ultimately publicised could be overprinted. The Beggarstaffs' *Chinaman* was to suffer a similar fate.

A chocolate-coloured border bearing the title of Hoyte's musical comedy was added to the Beggarstaffs' design by a printer's hack after the design left the artists' studio [25]. The practice of leaving the design and placing of lettering to the printer was not unusual at the time: it was still common when W. S. Rogers wrote his *Book of the Poster* in 1901. The procedure had its drawbacks, of course; Rogers observed that the final result was frequently out of balance, overweighted or simply spoilt by inappropriate and inharmonious characters. The *Trip to Chinatown* poster provides a good example of the dangers. As Nicholson remarked, the original design was 'mutilated' by the 'idiotic imitation of Chinese lettering'. The Beggarstaffs themselves would certainly have used more sober

25 Poster for a musical comedy entitled A *Trip to Chinatown* which incorporates the Beggarstaffs' *Chinaman* design. From a reproduction in M. Bauwens, etc., *Les Affiches étrangères illustrées*, 1897.

A TRIP TO CHINA TOWN
THE DANGERFIELD PRINTING Co.
LONDON.
COPYRIGHT REGISTERED No 26162.

25

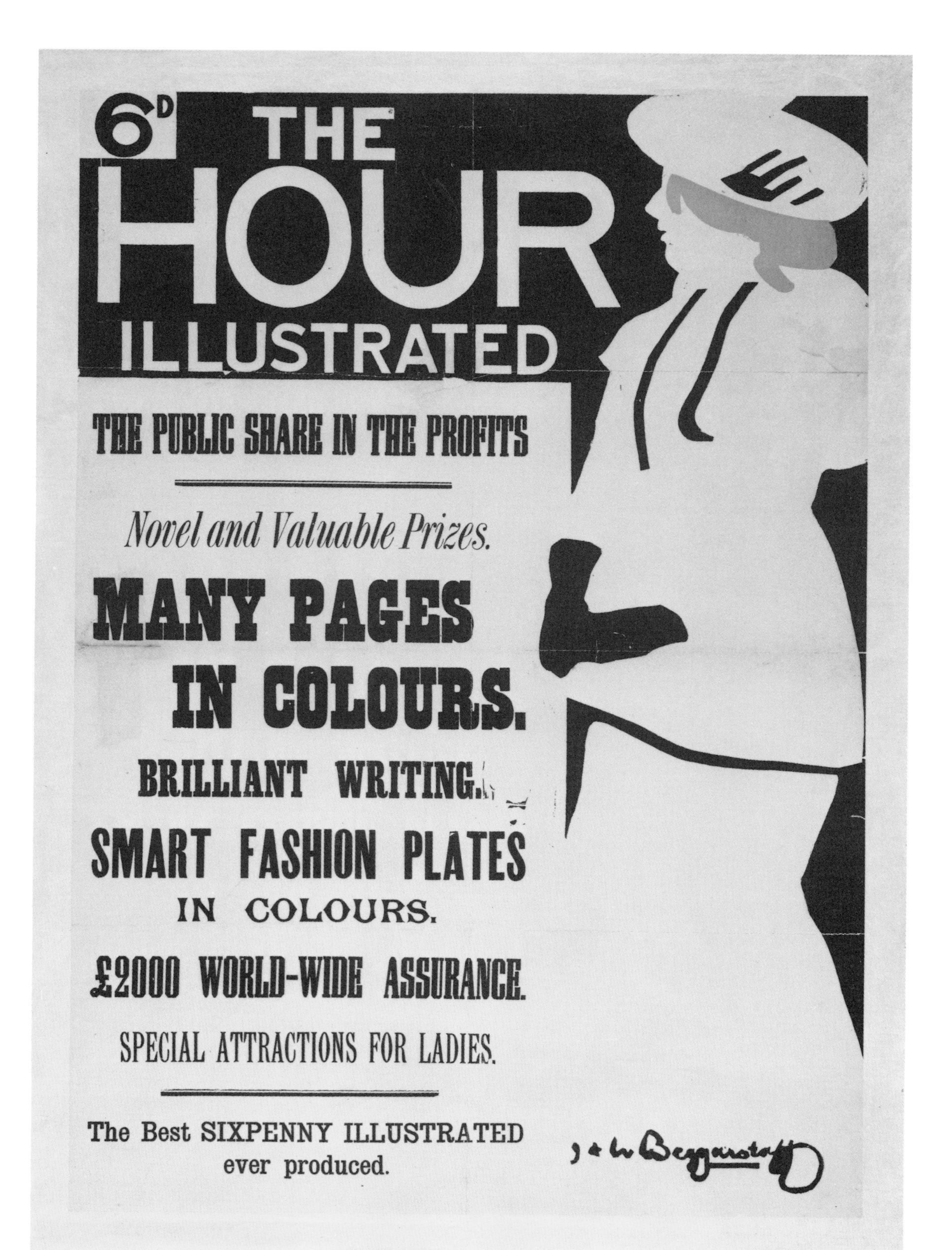
6D THE
HOUR
ILLUSTRATED
THE PUBLIC SHARE IN THE PROFITS
Novel and Valuable Prizes.
MANY PAGES
IN COLOURS.
BRILLIANT WRITING.
SMART FASHION PLATES
IN COLOURS.
£2000 WORLD-WIDE ASSURANCE.
SPECIAL ATTRACTIONS FOR LADIES.
The Best SIXPENNY ILLUSTRATED
ever produced.
J & W Beggarstaff

26a

26b J. & W. Beggarstaff, contents bill for *The Hour Illustrated*, 1895 (line block; 30 × 20 inches). A reproduction from Charles Hiatt's *Picture Posters* (1895) that appears to show the version of *The Hour* which was printed for collectors.

27 Cover of *The Hour Illustrated*, preliminary number, 27 March 1895. The journal illustrated here replaced an earlier magazine with the same title whose contents had a religious emphasis.

characters; and they might also have incorporated their lettering within the design. The poster as published was the only product of the Beggarstaff partnership to appear on the hoardings without a signature, evidence perhaps that the artists wished to dissociate themselves from what was a travesty of their work.

The Hour Illustrated [26a], one of the Beggarstaffs' smaller creations, is a two-colour contents bill or showcard designed to advertise a short-lived sixpenny illustrated weekly that first appeared in the spring of 1895 [27]. A rectangular space had to be provided for accompanying letterpress, and the appearance of this space when filled had therefore to be taken into account by the artists when developing their design.[18] Convention demanded representations of attractive young women in advertisements for illustrated journals, and here the Beggarstaffs followed established practice. The elegantly dressed, demurely posed lady they created is, however, much in contrast to the uninhibited female that Hardy drew

26a J. & W. Beggarstaff, contents bill for *The Hour Illustrated*, 1895 (line block; 30 × 20 inches). *By courtesy of the Board of Trustees of the Victoria and Albert Museum, London.*

to promote a very similar paper, *To-Day*. The 'pin-up' was never the Beggarstaffs' forte.

The Hour Illustrated contents bill takes as its starting point Greiffenhagen's showcard for another sixpenny illustrated paper: the *Pall Mall Budget* [5]. The way in which light on dark is cleverly alternated with dark on light in the Beggarstaff work owes something to Greiffenhagen's model, but the later work differs from the advertisement for the *Pall Mall Budget* in dispensing entirely with line. Here, in this showcard for *The Hour*, we see the first consistent use of the 'lost outline' that is a characteristic feature of some of the later Beggarstaff posters. In this instance, the Beggarstaffs were able to relate their simplified figure to plain sans-serif capitals from the beginning, and of course the design as a whole gains as a result. However, the work was not a total success. The dominance of white in the figure gives the impression of a photographic negative, and the sobriety of the showcard was a little out of keeping with the chatty tone of the journal. Like other Beggarstaff creations, it also lacked the vitality that is such an important ingredient in advertisements for popular topical papers. It nevertheless represents a significant stage in the development towards the Beggarstaffs' more mature designs of 1895 and 1896.

UNPUBLISHED DESIGNS FROM 1895

N AN ARTICLE PROBABLY WRITTEN IN THE SUMMER OF 1895 AND published in September of that year, Fish remarked that the Beggarstaffs' designs 'barely exceed a dozen in number'. The second half of 1895 was more productive, and by the end of the year, according to the man from *The Idler*, there was a 'huge collection' of finished and unfinished designs in the studio at Denham. The two young artists were producing far more work than they could possibly hope to sell.

Nicholson's records for 1895 (as quoted by Steen) refer to a number of designs which are described as either *Girl reading* or *Girl on a Sofa*. (The two titles appear to apply to the same project, and for convenience the designs are all referred to here as *Girl reading*.) The first of these designs was offered to Macmillan the publishers, but not accepted. The publishers were then offered a variant on the same theme, but this was also deemed unsatisfactory. Yet another design was submitted; but this too was rejected, and the Beggarstaffs' various submissions were all returned to them. The £20 that they were expecting to get for their work had to be written off.

28 J. & W. Beggarstaff, *Girl reading*, 1895 (design for a poster; dimensions unknown). From a reproduction in *The Studio*, September 1895.

28

Although none of the *Girl reading* designs survive, reproductions in contemporary journals document the appearance of two of them. An early version reproduced in *The Studio* [28] shows a young lady in a long white dress, black hat and black gloves seated on a chesterfield sofa. In the girl's hands is a book, described by Fish as red, but which appears from the reproduction in *The Studio* to be white. The shape of the girl's dress is not defined by an outline, but by the colours of the objects against which she is seen: a red cushion, the red and white stripes of the sofa, and the colour of the floor (grey-green, to judge from a subsequent version of the *Girl reading* theme). The design seen by the correspondent from *The Idler* was on brown paper, and so the area behind the sofa in the version reproduced in *The Studio* may have been brown rather than white. While Whistler's *Little White Girl* may have been in the Beggarstaffs' minds when they began work on their own girl in white, the psychologically remote figure we see in *The Studio* reproduction has nothing of the tender humanity of the American artist's painting. Taking their cue from French designers, the Beggarstaffs paid as much attention to the shape and size of the girl's hat as they did to its wearer.[19]

In a later *Girl reading* design, known from a reproduction in *The Poster* [V], the stripes on the chesterfield are broader and fewer. In this simplified version, the large hat plays a more important role than ever as an element in the composition, and the contrast between its oval shape and the adjoining square cushion is more apparent. Large ostrich-feather hats were much in Nicholson's mind in 1895, as a bookplate made for Phil May in that year shows [29]. A significant refinement in

29 William Nicholson, bookplate for Phil May, 1895. Ostrich-feather hats of the kind depicted in this woodcut were popular amongst the Cockney coster-girls that May loved to draw. *Private Collection.*

31 William Nicholson, *Queen Victoria*, 1897. Lithographic reproduction of a hand-coloured woodcut, the *New Review*, June 1897.

the later version of the design can be seen in the signature, the position and size of which allow it to contribute materially to the composition.

Why did Macmillan reject the Beggarstaffs' *Girl reading* designs? Perhaps the highly formalised character of these works was too novel. Perhaps, as a critic quoted by the man from *The Idler* remarked, the designs were regarded as representing a 'morbid French type'. The implication of this extraordinary description is that the *Girl reading* looked too much like the work of Toulouse-Lautrec – a comment which of course the artists (who admired Lautrec above all others) may well have taken as a compliment. Whatever the reason, Macmillan missed an opportunity to issue something that was a match for the publicity cards Beardsley was currently designing for their rivals, John Lane. The view that the Beggarstaffs' *Girl reading* was 'morbid' does not seem to have been shared by the critics in general; and a number of variations on the theme testify to the admiration of fellow artists. Ironically, among the designers who were influenced by the work was Beardsley himself [30].

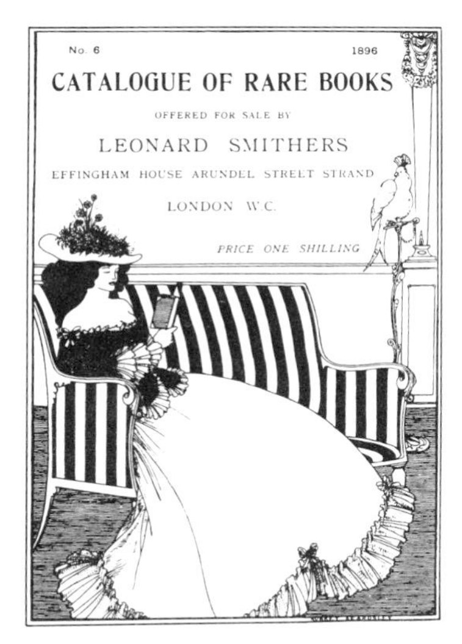

30 Aubrey Beardsley, wrapper for a catalogue issued by Leonard Smithers in 1896.

The anonymous article on the Beggarstaffs published in the January 1896 issue of *The Idler* refers to a 'fine design' of Queen Victoria. This was probably a speculative design made without any particular product in mind. The choice of subject was not an unusual one for a poster designer: advertisements for Sunlight

32

34

34 Pierre Bonnard, *Screen: nannies out walking; frieze of carriages*, 1899 (lithographs on four panels). Although Bonnard's lithographs date from 1899, the screeen was conceived as early as 1894, and a version in size colouring on canvas was painted in that year. *City Art Galleries, Leeds.*

33

32, 33 J. & W. Beggarstaff, *Children playing*, 1895 (decorative screen consisting of two panels, each 28 × 28 inches). *Andrew McIntosh Patrick Esq.*

Soap and other consumer goods show that many late-nineteenth-century manufacturers sought royal endorsement of their products. The *Queen Victoria* was never published, and no information exists on the dimensions of the now lost design. However, the article in *The Idler* records that it was on brown paper, and refers to the work as being in 'a quiet subdued style'. Apparently it depicted 'Her Majesty dressed in a street costume, and wearing a quiet little bonnet'. It is reasonable to assume from this description that the informal portrait of the Queen by Nicholson that was published in the June 1897 issue of the *New Review* [31] contains some echoes of this particular design.

The formal simplifications of the *Girl reading* designs are taken even further in the *Children playing*, a collage mounted on two panels which was almost certainly conceived as a decorative screen rather than a work with a commercial function [32, 33]. This work from 1895 is dominated by geometric forms such as the centrally placed circle (which represents a hoop) and the series of vertical lines (railings) that are arranged at intervals from one side of the composition to the other. The extent to which the artists' calculations were governed in this work by mathematical considerations is shown by the distance between adjoining railings, which is the same as the radius of the hoop. The subject matter and some of the motifs in this design derive from an idea for a four-panelled screen that Bonnard developed in 1894 and later lithographed [34]. However, the Beggarstaffs' collage lacks the gaiety and wit of its French model, and in general the rather severe effect of the work contrasts oddly with the innocence represented by the subject matter.

35 Paolo Uccello, *Battle of San Romano*, c. 1445. Nicholson was particularly fond of this panel painting, which offered examples of the use of profile and pattern. *Reproduced by courtesy of the Trustees, The National Gallery, London.*

An 'odd powerful thing representing a galloping Roundhead' [**VI**] is mentioned in *The Idler* article of 1896. This four-colour design combines some of the characteristics of the early Beggarstaff posters (the use of a strict profile, for example) with the highly simplified shapes that are to be found in the *Girl reading* and other designs. The pike in the foreground, whose presence can only be explained as a purely formal device, may have been inspired by similar objects in the painting *Battle of San Romano* by the fifteenth-century Italian artist Uccello [35]. The *Battle of San Romano*, which could be seen in the National Gallery, London, was a favourite of Nicholson's. 'How beautifully considered [Uccello's composition] is!' he exclaimed. 'I believe that no single lance could shift position by one fraction without endangering this perfect pattern.' The remark, quoted by Robert Nichols,[20] tells us much about the importance the Beggarstaffs attached to the placing of every detail in their own compositions.

The *Roundhead* title, employed by both the man from *The Idler* and Hiatt (1899), is an intriguing and perhaps misleading one. Pryde and Nicholson both loved Dumas, and the theme of this design is more likely to have been suggested by the French writer than by the English Civil War. The image itself is quite possibly an adaptation of a motif discovered in an etching by Callot – a printmaker whose work was admired and used by the two artists.[21] Where would the lettering have been placed in the Beggarstaffs' mysterious *Roundhead*? What could it possibly have been intended to advertise? Is the reproduction in *The Poster* true to the original design? The contours around horse, harness, rider, banner and cloud are uncharacteristically crude, indicating an imperfect transcription of the original design.

It is possible that one or both of the *Roundhead* and *Queen Victoria* designs from 1895 were submitted to (and rejected by) advertisers, but no evidence of this survives.

I J. & W. Beggarstaff, *Hamlet*, 1894 (stencil; $67\frac{3}{8} \times 28\frac{7}{8}$ inches). *Collection, The Museum of Modern Art, New York. Gift of the Lauder Foundation, Leonard and Evelyn Lauder Fund, Jack Banning, and by exchange.*

II J. & W. Beggarstaff, *Becket*, 1894 (design for a poster; 69$\frac{1}{6}$ × 43$\frac{3}{4}$ inches). *Ellen Terry Memorial Museum, Tenterden.*

III J. & W. Beggarstaff, *Kassama Corn Flour*, 1894 (lithograph; 60 × 40 inches). *Kunstgewerbemuseum, Cologne.*

"KASSAMA"
CORN
FLOUR
J & W Beggarstaff
Henderson & Co
Printers Copyright

THE DANGERFIELD
PRINTING Co
LONDON.
COPYRIGHT REGISTERED No 26162.

IV J. & W. Beggarstaff, *Chinaman*, 1894/5 (design; $80\frac{1}{2} \times 54$ inches). *By courtesy of the Board of Trustees of the Victoria and Albert Museum, London.*

V J. & W. Beggarstaff, *Girl reading*, 1895 (design for a poster; dimensions unknown). From a reproduction in *The Poster*, February 1899.

VI J. & W. Beggarstaff, *Roundhead*, 1895 (design for a poster; dimensions unknown). From a reproduction in *The Poster*, February 1899.

VII J. & W. Beggarstaff, *Don Quixote*, 1895 (design for a poster; dimensions unknown). From a reproduction in *The Poster*, August–September 1898.

VIII J. & W. Beggarstaff, *Harper's Magazine*, 1895 (lithograph; 85 × 76 inches). From a reproduction in *The Poster*, February 1899.

IX J. & W. Beggarstaff, *Cinderella*, 1895 (design for a poster; dimensions unknown). From a reproduction in *The Poster*, February 1899.

X J. & W. Beggarstaff, *Rowntree's Elect Cocoa*, 1896 (lithograph; 38 × 28⅝ inches). *By courtesy of the Board of Trustees of the Victoria and Albert Museum, London.*

XI James Pryde, *William Nicholson*, probably 1897 (lithograph; $8\frac{1}{4} \times 5\frac{3}{4}$ inches). Supplement in *The Studio*, December 1897.

XII William Nicholson, *James Pryde*, 1899 (woodcut; $7\frac{3}{4} \times 5\frac{3}{4}$ inches). Supplement in *The Studio*, July 1901.

Don Quixote

HE *Don Quixote*, PERHAPS THE FINEST OF ALL THE BEGGARSTAFFS' creations, was intended as an advertisement for a new stage production entitled *A Chapter from Don Quixote*, which opened at the Lyceum Theatre on 4 May 1895 with Henry Irving in the title role. The play, founded on an incident in Cervantes, consisted of two scenes contrived out of the first act of an adaptation by W. G. Wills. The production was not sufficient for an evening's entertainment on its own, and it was presented to the public as part of a triple bill of one-act plays. A minor event in the history of the Lyceum, *A Chapter from Don Quixote* was completely overshadowed during its brief run by one of the pieces that accompanied it: Arthur Conan Doyle's *Story of Waterloo*. As an event in Irving's career, it is remembered largely on account of a happy coincidence, for it was while the actor was playing the fictional role of the 'Knight of the Woeful Countenance' that the knighthood conferred on him by Queen Victoria was announced.

Pryde and Nicholson made three separate *Don Quixote* designs. The first does not survive, but is reproduced among other places in the September 1895 issue of *The Studio* [36] and Hiatt's *Picture Posters* (1895). This first version was later revised in a large four-colour collage: a work which lay rolled up in Nicholson's studio for many years before being acquired by the Victoria and Albert Museum [37]. This, the second version, did not meet the Beggarstaffs' exacting standards, and was superseded in turn by a now lost design first published in January 1896 **[VII]**. It was this third and final version, a work in which the Beggarstaffs reveal their growing assurance in the handling of line and form, that was eventually presented by the artists to Irving.

All three of the Beggarstaffs' designs show the figure of Don Quixote seated in profile on a white horse. The knight's head is light brown, with shadow being used for the first time to convey a sense of form. His armour and shield are a darker brown, the three-dimensional nature of the forms in this area being simply and cleverly indicated by highlights of the kind that are exploited in some of Nicholson's early woodcuts. But nowhere is the economy of means in this astonishing work more evident than in Don Quixote's horse. While the legs and hind parts of this animal are defined by line alone, the creature's head and neck are a mere pale silhouette broken only by an abbreviated representation of a head-collar. Our ability to read this silhouette depends on the presence of the dark windmill against which it is seen. In Cervantes, Don Quixote imagined the windmills with which he did battle to be giants, and so the Beggarstaffs made their mill as large as possible. The two-dimensional character of this object (which recalls a painted stage flat rather than a real building) and the implication of a low viewpoint make the *Don Quixote* the most theatrical of the Beggarstaffs' works for the theatre.

In its use of both light and dark silhouettes, the *Don Quixote* echoes the principle of varying contrasts already encountered in the *Girl reading* designs. A light-toned ground is now preferred to a brown ground, in order to exploit the effect of these contrasts to the full. Here, as elsewhere at this date, the artists were presumably anticipating lithographic reproduction of their work; but their use of profile and silhouette shows their continuing attachment to a style originally developed for stencil reproduction. The angular outline of the head and neck of

36 J. & W. Beggarstaff, *Don Quixote*, 1895 (design for a poster; dimensions unknown). The first of the *Don Quixote* designs. From a reproduction in *The Studio*, September 1895.

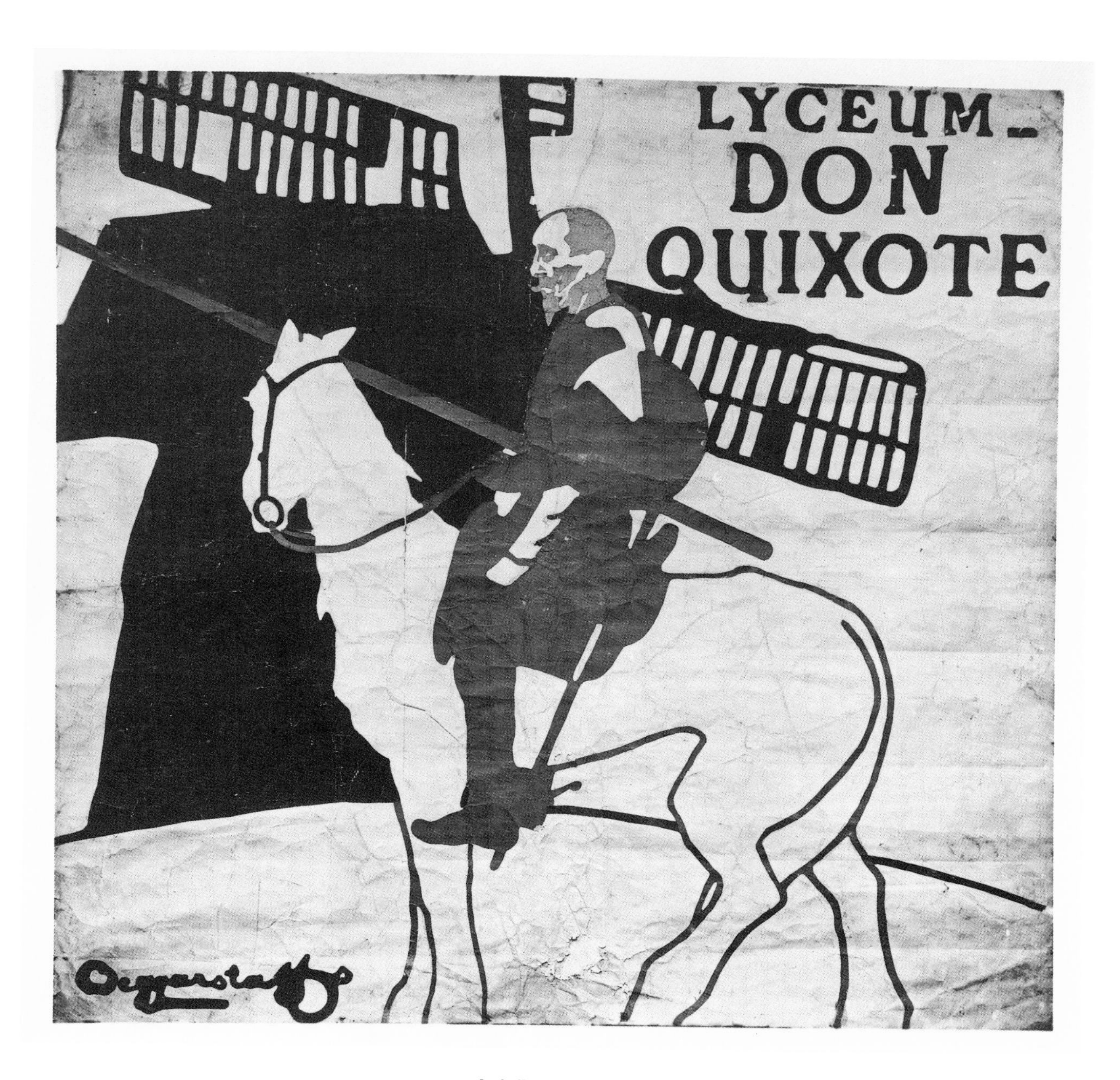

37 J. & W. Beggarstaff, *Don Quixote*, 1895 (design for a poster; 76 × 77¼ inches). The second of the *Don Quixote* designs. *By courtesy of the Board of Trustees of the Victoria and Albert Museum.*

Don Quixote's steed – clear evidence of the use of knife or scissors – also recalls the early 'stencil style'.

During their slow, painstaking progress towards a formal solution that satisfied them, the artists subjected their composition to rigorous simplification, the results of which are most clearly seen in the sails of the mill. In its final, definitive form, the work is an object lesson in how to achieve maximum variety and contrast while at the same time keeping detail to an absolutely irreducible minimum. As in the *Children playing*, the artists reveal a preoccupation with regular forms (for example, the pole of unvarying width that is depicted in place of the lance actually used on stage, and the segment of the arc of a circle that stands for the horizon), but the geometric basis of these forms is now less obtrusive.

The *Don Quixote* is the earliest large-scale work by the Beggarstaffs known today in which the lettering was conceived as part of the composition from the very beginning. Although already an indispensable complement to the imagery, the lettering lacks emphasis in the first version of the design. In the second and third versions, however, a heavier typeface not only functions as an integral part of the work, but has a character and weight that are in complete harmony with the imagery. This lettering is quite different from that in such earlier works as the *Kassama Corn Flour* poster. Now, in place of letters based on forms cut from paper with scissors, we find letters drawn in imitation of old English typefaces of the seventeenth and eighteenth centuries.[22]

The *Don Quixote* is the first of the Beggarstaff works to show the full impact on Pryde and Nicholson of Toulouse-Lautrec. The young artists' admiration for Lautrec was boundless at this time (Pryde is quoted in *The Idler* as saying that the Frenchman was 'one of the few artists who understand what a poster is and should be'). They had of course come across Lautrec's work at the Westminster Aquarium the previous year, but it was not until the *Don Quixote* project was under way that the experience of the French artist's posters bore fruit. Lautrec's *Moulin Rouge – La Goulue* of 1891 [20] was a major influence. This poster, exhibited at the Aquarium in 1894, showed how flat, ungradated masses could be combined with line; and how light and dark forms could be contrasted. Lautrec also demonstrated the decorative potential of a simple black mass (sometimes termed a 'black blot'), and the usefulness of an abbreviated form (i.e., a form cut by the edge of the composition) as a means of enhancing the pictorial interest of a work.

T WAS REPORTED IN *THE IDLER* THAT ONE OF THE *DON QUIXOTE* designs was purchased by Henry Irving, and this was confirmed by Pryde, who claimed in his autobiographical essay that Irving not only commissioned the two artists to work on this project, but paid for the final product. According to Steen, Irving gave the young artists double the £50 they asked – a magnanimous gesture that would hardly have been justified by an unsolicited design.[23] But can Irving really have commissioned a work which called attention to only one of the three plays in the Lyceum's triple bill, and the least important of them at that? As we have already seen, Irving did not normally commission pictorial posters, and if he did so on this occasion he presumably intended to send the Beggarstaffs' design to the printers. In the event, however, the design was never used. As with the *Becket* design, the reasons are unclear. Bella, who said that Irving took the design to the USA, '*pour l'essayer sur le chien*', reported that the actor-manager felt it to be too bold for use in England. The view that Pryde expressed some years later was that the decision to discard the design was made 'because the play failed and was soon withdrawn'; but neither this, nor the observation quoted by Steen that the work was not used 'on score of expenses and short run' (the source of this quote was not given), is very convincing. Perhaps the crucial factor in the decision not to publish the work was the Don's lack of resemblance to Irving – a shortcoming which, it was said, displeased the great actor.

If the Beggarstaffs' Don Quixote was not based on Irving, who was the model? Was it possibly Joseph Conrad, who was very much in the public eye in 1895? In his autobiographical *Personal Record*, Conrad referred to Don Quixote as a source of inspiration; and in the summer of 1898 Nicholson sent the Polish writer a woodcut adaptation of one of the Beggarstaffs' *Don Quixote* designs. However, his moustache and beard apart, Conrad bears too little resemblance to the Beggarstaffs' Quixote to make him a strong candidate, and a more likely model is perhaps the artists' mentor, Joseph Pennell, who had recently returned from an extended trip to Spain [15]. There are certainly reminiscences of Pennell in the head of the Beggarstaffs' knight; but one must not make too much of them, and the safest conclusion is probably that the head of the Don is largely invention: a gaunt, reflective Spanish head of a kind that seemed, to the Beggarstaffs, to fit the *gravitas* of their conception better than the grotesque and clownish appearance that Irving assumed for this production.[24]

Irving's performances always received publicity, and his appearance as Don Quixote was no exception. Some could find no fault with the great man, praising his ability to make Don Quixote come to life upon the stage. 'The very figure,' wrote Irving's biographer, Brereton, 'tall and spare, with frail, pointed beard, arched eyebrows, and dreamy, absent look, combined in making a lasting portrait. But he succeeded in depicting Don Quixote in more than appearance. He presented the chivalry of the character, with all its gentle feeling, all its honourable purpose.'[25] Others, however, were less impressed; and indeed it may be said that in general *A Chapter from Don Quixote* pleased only those playgoers who had never read Cervantes. Critics could not fail to notice how Irving, blowing off steam after months of playing Wolsey, Becket and King Arthur, attempted to distract attention from the poverty of the text by indulging in extravagantly comic antics, such as using his sword to turn over the pages of *Amadis de Gaul* and trying to carry a ten-foot lance erect through a seven-foot doorway. 'Never was there such a disappointment as Mr Irving's performance,' wrote Archer. 'He pitches his Don Quixote throughout in the key of farce; whereas he ought clearly to be a figure of romance.'[26] Irving's light-hearted interpretation of his role is clearly illustrated in an engraving after H. M. Paget which was published on the cover of *The Graphic* [38].

Believing that Cervantes was worthy of more serious treatment than he received at Irving's hands, the Beggarstaffs made changes in their poster design to the production's scenery and props as well as to the appearance and demeanour of Don Quixote himself. Their windmill was introduced in place of the village pump that occupied the stage in the second scene; and the authentic looking Rosinante – all skin and bone, but a noble animal for all that – was substituted for a robust

38 H. M. Paget, *Don Quixote inditing a letter to Dulcinea while Sancho Panza is buckling on his armour*. Drawing of a scene from Henry Irving's production of *Don Quixote* at the Lyceum Theatre. *The Graphic*, 11 May 1895.

and well-covered steed (a veteran of the London stage much given to flatulence) that Irving had had painted with counterfeit ribs and bones to give the effect of emaciation. The result was a design of great dignity – a quality not usually associated with the garish theatrical posters of the 1890s. The poster was, in short, better than the play. It was much admired in England and abroad [39], but in 1895 it would have done little to prepare visitors to the Lyceum for Irving's production, and it is perhaps hardly surprising that it was never published.

39 P. Véryne, *France admiring the Beggarstaffs' 'Don Quixote'*. From a reproduction in *The Poster*, November 1899. The Beggarstaffs had an enthusiastic following on the Continent.

HARPER'S MAGAZINE

THE BEGGARSTAFFS EXPERIENCED SUCCESSES AS WELL AS FAILURES during 1895. The most notable of these successes followed the creation, around the same time as the *Don Quixote*, of a poster featuring one of Her Majesty's yeomen of the guard [41, **VIII**]. Beefeaters were not a subject new to advertising (for many years during the early nineteenth century one could be seen on a signboard outside a menagerie in the Strand); but to advertisers of the 1890s the motif had a new appeal. Historical associations linked it with tradition – the buying habits of earlier generations are constantly invoked in advertisements of the period – and the motif's 'Englishness' identified it with the proven superiority of British goods.

It is a masterly work. The Beggarstaffs' Beefeater turns his back on the viewer, preserving for himself a degree of anonymity that is a characteristic of figures in the two artists' earlier posters. The natural grace of the man's stance (an echo of Velázquez here) is contrasted with the rigidity of the lance that splits the composition. Economy of means is as much the guiding principle in the representation of this figure as it is in the *Girl reading* and *Hour* designs – so much so, indeed, that the viewer must decipher the picture rather than read it. A few visual clues such as shoes, garters and hat are easily recognised, but everything else is a mere suggestion: a shadow on the face; a few bands of black on the costume; a hint of outline here and there; and important 'drop-out' areas of white in the region of the collar and hat buckle.

In making the entire background the same colour as the Beefeater himself, the Beggarstaffs' took an idea they had begun to explore in *Girl reading* a stage further, in the process creating (quite unintentionally) the effect of a figure seen through mist or fog. A token outline is introduced at selected points; and in a few places decorative bands on the costume help define the borders of the figure. However, the contours of the Beefeater must otherwise be reconstructed in the viewer's

41 J. & W. Beggarstaff, *Harper's Magazine*, 1895 (lithograph; 85 × 76 inches). From a reproduction in M. Bauwens, etc., *Les affiches étrangères illustrées*, Paris, 1897. The differences between this version of the *Harper's Magazine* poster and that reproduced in fig. 40 lie mainly in the lettering. The selective approach to line and form, and the use of the same colour for figure and background derive from Beardsley's Avenue Theatre poster.

HARPER'S
is the largest
and most popular
MAGAZINE
yet owing to its
enormous sale
and in spite of
the great expense
of production,
the price is
STILL
ONE SHILLING
The Artistic Supply Co. Ltd.
Amberley House W.C.
Printed by Stafford & Co Netherfield Nottm
Copyrighted in America. 1895.

41

mind. The resulting configuration, in which line and pattern are everything and masses play almost no part, has the beauty of true simplicity. As always, the apparent effortlessness of the exercise is deceptive.

Puns were very popular in advertisements of the period, and the Beggarstaffs decided that their Beefeater would be suitably occupied encouraging the public to eat extract of beef. It was a logical decision. Competition between manufacturers of beef extract was keen; and the Beggarstaffs could not have failed to notice that some of the firms concerned were still using purely typographical advertisements. Manufacturers whose posters contained a pictorial element occasionally introduced a modern note in the form of a pretty girl expatiating to passers-by on the qualities of the product (*'Really, nothing could be nicer than—'*); but bulls, and archaic emblems such as Hercules and the Lion, were still very common. Calling on one of the many manufacturers of beef extract, the Beggarstaffs pinned their original design up on the wall of the small room into which they were shown. 'After a while,' recalled Pryde, 'the art editor or manager or whatever he called himself, a dear old gentleman rather like Father Christmas in appearance, came into the room.' The Beggarstaffs' hopes of a quick sale rose, only to be dashed. 'He gave the poster one glance,' said Pryde, 'and went out of the room without saying anything.'

Undeterred, the Beggarstaffs offered their design to Sir George Alexander, a former employee of Irving's, who in the 1890s was manager of the St James's Theatre. Gilbert and Sullivan's *Yeoman of the Guard* was playing at the St James's; but Sir George was quite happy with the Beefeater already on the hoardings outside his theatre, and he turned the Beggarstaffs' design down. Pryde and Nicholson decided to take the design to the Artistic Supply Company, and it was this agency that found a buyer for it. Harper's, one of the pioneers of the artistic poster in the USA, were looking for an effective means of advertising the European edition of their magazine, and a decorative rather than illustrative design such as the Beggarstaffs' Beefeater suited their purpose. In this way, a design initially created with beef extract in mind was ultimately used to promote a magazine: an outcome which must have confirmed Pryde and Nicholson in their opinion that in advertising it was more important to be striking than relevant.

The Beggarstaffs insisted on retaining responsibility for the lettering in the *Harper's* design; and Nicholson was later to say that he and his partner took infinite trouble over this part. In placing the text in a panel that embraced the design on two of its sides, the artists followed an established convention. However, they managed to achieve a more harmonious relationship between image and lettering than we find in the combinations of lithographic reproduction and letterpress of earlier artists. The Beefeater's red background is extended in such a way as to form a frame for the text, and this helps to knit the two main components of the design together. Hand-painting of the lettering (as opposed to the use of letterpress) enabled the Beggarstaffs to achieve both a satisfactory relationship between black and white within the panel, and the precise 'weight' that was needed to balance the image. The lettering itself shows the influence of eighteenth-century playbills. This is evident from the character of the typeface, the short lines composed of only a few words, the use of a rule, and the alternation on successive lines of capital and lower-case letters. As before, the signature – on the lower left – is an important element in the design.

Pryde and Nicholson seem to have experimented to some extent with geometry in the *Harper's Magazine* design, for a part or the whole of the composi-

normally be expected from that quarter.) And of course the Beggarstaffs were held in high regard by fellow artists. The April 1896 issue of *The Studio* was one of several journals to identify Pryde and Nicholson as pioneers of certain changes that were now taking place in poster design. A. S. Hartrick wrote in the catalogue of the second Aquarium exhibition about the 'triumph of the silhouette', and related how the older principles of excessive relief, much detail, and many printings were now being abandoned. The role that the Beggarstaffs had played in helping to bring these changes about was widely recognised.

The Beggarstaffs' contributions to the 1896 exhibition enhanced their reputation still further. A measure of the esteem in which the work they sent to the exhibition was held is reflected in the readiness of reviewers to lavish praise on the two men's *unpublished* designs – some of which had of course been rejected by advertisers. An example is provided by the *Don Quixote* design, which attracted much attention at the Aquarium. Hartrick regarded this particular work as the most artistic of the Beggarstaffs' contributions to the exhibition; and a reviewer in the 1 April 1896 issue of *The Sketch* observed that it was 'as fine a piece of imaginative work as was ever designed for a hoarding'. Macfall (1896/1) wrote: 'I have never seen a canvas more thoroughly catch and concentrate the spirit of a whole work of imaginative prose so perfectly . . . the quaintness of Cervantes' hand has passed to the hands of these men, and the old-world air of the book is marvellously realised in this thing. Here are the decorative limits of the poster carried to their furthest, and the beauty of the accomplishment is a marvel to me'.

The artists' published work – *Harper's Magazine* and *Cinderella* – held many of the visitors to the exhibition spellbound. Macfall, who spoke of the latter as the triumph of the show, described it as 'one of the most beautiful things that has ever adorned our walls'. This xenophobic reviewer believed that beside such work the efforts of Chéret were almost cheap and commonplace. The Beggarstaffs had 'all the quaintness, all the original point of view that the best French poster designers, such as Lautrec, have shown without the French artists' over-enforcement of the grotesque and of their too pronounced love of the risky. And we have a capacity for daring, yet well-disciplined colour harmony which far outdistances any one else who has yet designed posters.' When it came to comparisons with English artists, Macfall had no doubts about the Beggarstaffs' supremacy. As Hartrick had already noticed, Hardy had lately been attempting to find a compromise between the old theatrical poster style and the new; and a comparison of the Beggarstaffs' *Cinderella* with Hardy's bill for the same production (also at the Aquarium) was sufficient to prove to him that Pryde and Nicholson had usurped Hardy's position as the leading light of English poster design.

The April 1896 issue of *The Studio* recorded the influence which the Beggarstaffs had exerted on many of the works submitted by fellow exhibitors at the second Aquarium exhibition. This influence was, it seems, exceeded only by that of Beardsley. Gordon Craig was among the artists who were bowled over by the Beggarstaffs' contributions to Bella's second exhibition. Renting a room over a pork butcher's shop while on tour in Chatham during the spring of 1896, he worked alone on some posters 'à la Beggarstaff'. Craig was honest enough to admit that the work he produced in the second half of the 1890s [47], like that of others who fell under the Beggarstaffs' spell, was 'utter imitation'.

The growing celebrity of Pryde and Nicholson led artists to produce parodies of their work as well as imitations. An example reproduced here is a drawing by Jack Yeats which draws attention to the Beggarstaffs' liking for asymmetrical

47 Edward Gordon Craig, poster for *The Dome*, c. 1898. The first number of *The Poster Collector's Circular* (January 1899) describes this work as 'conceived in the Beggarstaff vein of extreme simplicity, though not altogether Beggarstaffian in treatment'. The figure depicted is Henry Irving.

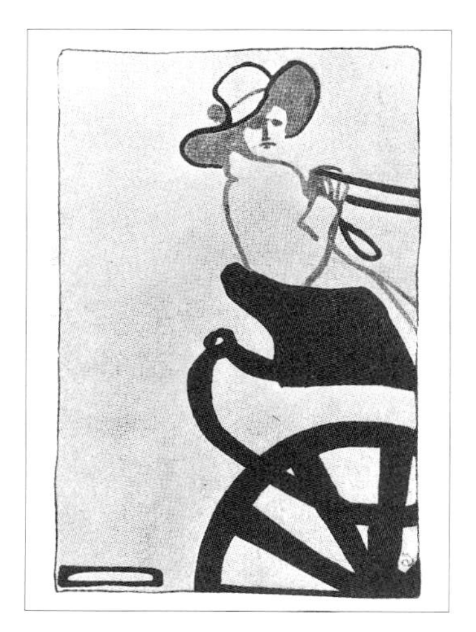

48 Jack Yeats, *The Beggarstaff Style*. Drawing published in *The Poster*, August 1900.

compositions and cut-off forms [48]. This drawing was not intended to be a work of art, but it nevertheless suggests that many of the subtleties of the Beggarstaffs' designs were lost even on their admirers.

Meanwhile, the prices of the Beggarstaffs' published work were on the increase, reflecting the continuing interest of collectors. The *Harper's Magazine* poster sold at 8 shillings at the Aquarium; the *Cinderella* at 10 shillings. These were double the average prices paid for Lautrec posters at the exhibition. From every point of view, then, the future still looked fairly promising. 'My only fear,' Macfall remarked prophetically, 'is that the average business man is so utterly wanting in the art sense that he will likely not appreciate what is best when he sees it.'

Rowntree's Elect Cocoa

In 1896, Rowntree's of York, shortly to become a limited company, were looking for ways of updating their advertising, and the Artistic Supply Company suggested to the Beggarstaffs that they submit a design for a poster to the firm. This design was to be specifically for Rowntree's, and lettering was therefore to be included from the beginning. The Beggarstaffs' design, which was probably produced in the second half of 1896, was submitted and approved. It was published in two versions: one measuring about 3 feet in height [**X**], and a larger version about 13 feet high made up of a number of separate sheets. The first reference to this new work is in the 25 February 1897 issue of *Figaro*, where Pryde and Nicholson described it as 'our latest thing'. At this date the poster was already on display in the provinces, but it had not been seen in London. According to Furst, the Beggarstaffs' fee was £30.

Rowntree's wanted to increase the sales of their strong, nutritious cocoa. How was this to be done? Most artists of the time would have chosen to draw the attention of the public to the economy of the product (120 breakfast cups could be filled from a 3-shilling tin) or its quality (all the appetising and refreshing properties of the choicest cocoa beans are preserved in it unimpaired, claimed the manufacturers). However, the Beggarstaffs knew that reasoned arguments do not catch the eye. Only an image could do this; and, if the image was sufficiently striking, it was worth more than any dissertation on the product's merits.

The image the Beggarstaffs created for Rowntrees consisted of a simple group of three figures in period costume. The dominant figure in this group (the man in a black hat and black jacket) has a cup beside him – the only pictorial reference to the product advertised apart from the same man's check waistcoat of pinky-brown (i.e., cocoa colour). Behind this man are two others: the three figures forming a beautifully integrated group that testifies to the developing sophistication of the Beggarstaffs' compositions. The costumes of these men had a picturesque appeal for both artists; and they were also justified by established practice, for beverage advertisements frequently pointed to the preferences of previous generations as examples worth following. As in the *Cinderella* poster, areas of flat, ungradated colour (here, black and pinky-brown) are combined with economical use of line (a reticent olive-green). The dominance of black over the other colours in this work probably reflects Nicholson's increasing activity as a maker of woodcuts. The accompanying lettering is kept to a minimum. Nowhere in the Beggarstaffs' *oeuvre* are image and lettering in more perfect harmony, and nowhere is the effect of simplicity and balance achieved with less obvious effort.

Many people praised the advertisement – including Rowntree's themselves, who described it as a 'striking poster' made by artists who have 'executed many quaint works of this kind, but none more original than this'. Pryde's friend Martin Shaw went so far as to say that the work 'almost made me drink cocoa – which, in common with G. K. Chesterton (and, I suspect, the Beggarstaff Brothers), I detest'.[39] Initially, however, people were taken aback by it, not least by the Beggarstaffs' use of blank spaces around the figures. The novelty of this aspect of the work is reflected in the well-known song-writer Richard Morton's satirical poem *On the wall. A poster dialogue*, where the foreground figure feels obliged to excuse and explain these blank spaces – which he calls 'my special beauty'. And in a ballad entitled *The Blind Beggarstaff of Bethnal Green* Morton considered a fault the Beggarstaffs had perhaps not foreseen: the speed with which the pristine beauty of their work was sullied when exposed to the hazards of the street:

A splotch of mud on a Beggarstaff Man,
A splotch and that is all:
But it blinds the eye of the Cocoa Man
On a Bethnal Green dead wall.

Perhaps the least justified of the criticisms of the Beggarstaffs' poster were those which centred on the work's so-called 'sobriety'. In his *On the wall* dialogue, Morton accused the Beggarstaffs of making the 'Praise-God-barebones' figure in the foreground one of puritanical gloom. The remark seems to arise at least partly from the mistaken assumption that the figure represents Joseph Rowntree, the founder of the cocoa firm, who was an ardent Quaker. (Rowntree was also an ardent temperance reformer – a fact crucial to Morton's ironic description of an incident in which a bill-sticker covers the *Rowntree's* poster with an advertisement for Bass Beer.) The stigma of sobriety was of course undeserved, being based on no more than the Beggarstaffs' liking for black and the absence from their posters of the kind of animated gaiety that characterised Hardy's work.

Rowntree's, recognising that many members of the public were more than a little baffled by this cryptic poster, sensibly attempted to turn what was seen as a weakness into a strength by claiming that the work was a 'puzzle picture'. Such pictures were not uncommon in advertising at this date, and they were regarded as quite effective. 'It is good to puzzle people,' asserted Gleeson White in his lecture on posters to the Society of Arts in January 1896. 'If they think over the puzzle and find it out, their trouble and cleverness helps to fix the fact in their memory.' The *Rowntree's* poster seemed to perform the role of a 'teaser' rather well. As Stewart

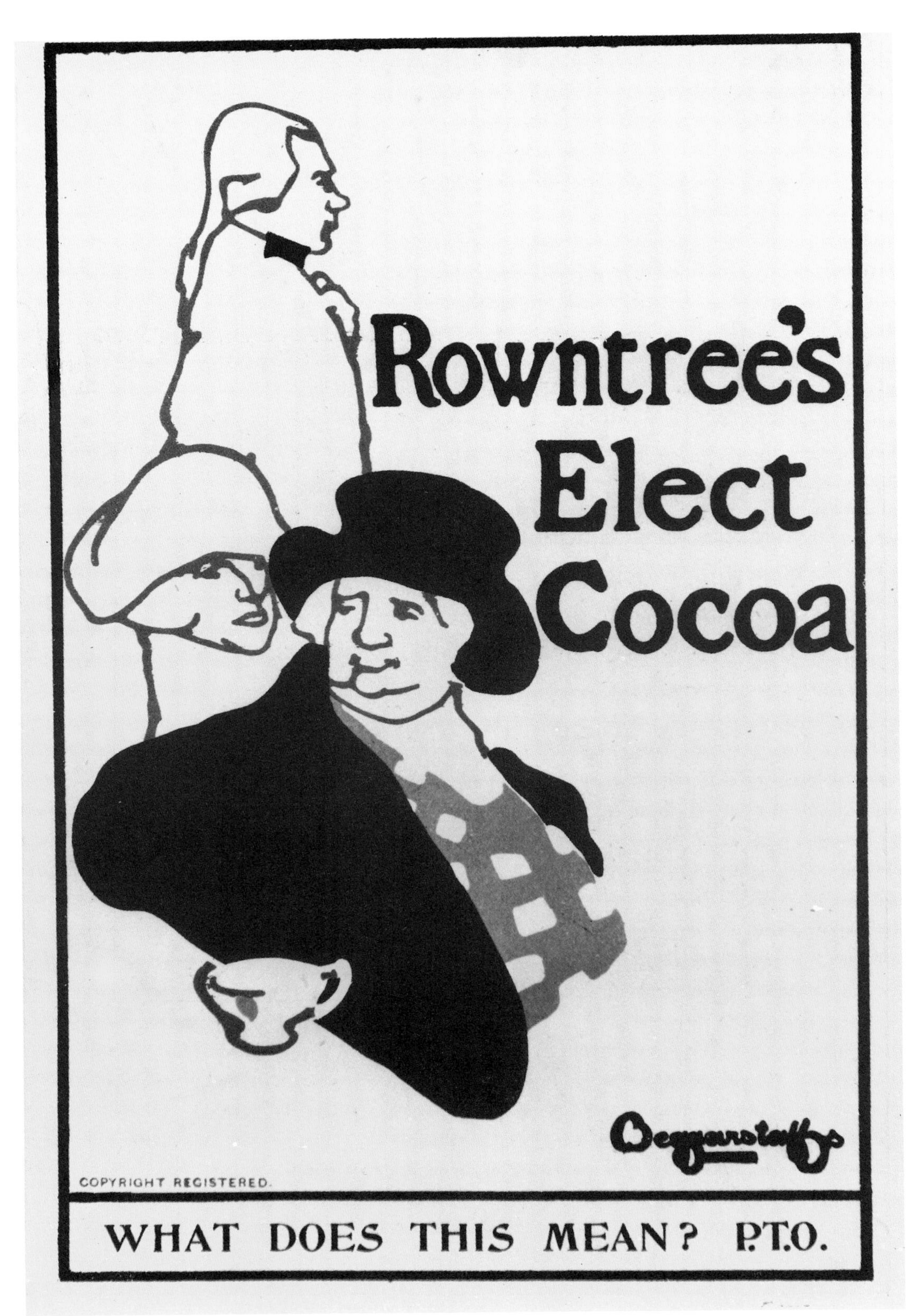
Rowntree's
Elect
Cocoa
Beggarstaffs
COPYRIGHT REGISTERED.
WHAT DOES THIS MEAN? P.T.O.

49

Browne observed in 1899, 'The public never overlook a good thing: not even Rowntree's excellent puzzle poster, designed by the Beggarstaffs. Everyone has seen that and made a note of Rowntree's, which, of course, is the whole duty of a poster.'[40]

Rowntree's now began to offer prizes for the best solution to the poster's meaning [49]. The public responded, but an advertisement in the 5 March 1898 issue of *British Weekly* reveals that none of the entrants in the competition really hit the mark. The manufacturers thereupon announced that the artists' intention had simply been to represent three generations of sturdy British types of men, the latest comer enjoying a privilege denied to his ancestors – a refreshing cup of Rowntree's Elect Cocoa.

Rowntree's 'solution' to their so-called 'puzzle picture' does not convince: the costumes of the three men do not identify them as belonging to three different generations; and in any case the men portrayed all appear to belong to an era predating that of Joseph Rowntree (who was not born until 1836). It seems certain, therefore, that the manufacturer's interpretation of the poster's meaning was published without any reference to the artists. The Beggarstaffs themselves probably did not have any specific 'meaning' in mind, their purpose being simply to allude to a single era of English history into which their ancestors might have been born. The probability that the figures represented are contemporary with each other is confirmed by a letter from Gordon Craig to Derek Hudson dated 16 April 1948. Craig observed in this letter that the man wearing the black hat represents Charles James Fox (1749–1806), while the tall figure at the back is modelled on William Pitt (1759–1806). Craig's recollections can be supplemented with the observation that the central figure is Lord Nelson (1758–1805).[41]

The *Rowntree's Elect Cocoa* poster, the largest of all the Beggarstaffs' published

49 Undated reproduction of J. & W. Beggarstaff's *Rowntree's Elect Cocoa* (process engraving; $8\frac{1}{2} \times 5\frac{1}{2}$ inches). Rowntree's answer to the question posed on the front of this reduced facsimile is printed on the back.

50 *Rowntree's Illustrated Calendar for 1899.* The modernity of the imagery that the Beggarstaffs created for Rowntree's is more apparent when seen in conjunction with earlier advertisements for the firm.

advertisements, soon became the most familiar. Fox and his companions remained in circulation for many years, appearing in a wide variety of forms on everything from the huge, multi-sheet versions of the poster down to small, pocket-size calendars [50]. The enamel version of the advertisement [51] could still be seen outside the grocers' shops of England half a century later. Sadly, however, the work was to be the last important creation of the partnership. Pryde and Nicholson collaborated again, but subsequent projects did not reach the hoardings.

The *Quiver* Competition

A NUMBER OF POSTER COMPETITIONS WERE HELD DURING THE 1890s. The Beggarstaffs did not normally take part in these, but in late 1896 or early 1897 they entered a competition organised by the publishers Cassell's for a design to advertise *The Quiver*, an illustrated monthly magazine for 'Sunday and general reading'.

The Beggarstaffs' *Quiver* design was one of 234 entries in the Cassell's competition. It has not survived, but it was reported by Hiatt (1899) to represent a man in black tights with an orange feather in his hat on a green background. The man was presumably an archer. According to Hiatt, the design was ranked among the Beggarstaffs' best productions. However, it was not only unplaced in the competition, it was not even among the score or so entries that received a commendation. The panel of judges appears to have included the editor of the *Magazine of Art*, M. H. Spielmann, who was less than enthusiastic about the Beggarstaffs' work, and the disappointing outcome could perhaps have been expected.

The winner of the £75 first prize in the *Quiver* competition was Henry Holiday, who had submitted a restrained design featuring two bow-bearing females in classical robes. Holiday was quoted in the May 1897 issue of the *Magazine of Art* as saying that he believed posters with powerful oppositions of colour had been 'done and overdone', and this point of view clearly helped his submission win favour with the judges at the expense of designs which featured such arresting contrasts as orange and green. 'In awarding the first prize to Mr Holiday's composition,' the *Magazine of Art* announced in May 1897, 'consideration was given to the fact that there are now so many posters of the "shouting" order that one so refined yet firm in

51 Enamel version of J. & W. Beggarstaffs' *Rowntree's Elect Cocoa*.

51

52

design and delicate in colour would be more likely to "tell" on a hoarding than one which followed the current vogue.'

The *Quiver* episode was a setback, but it can hardly be described as an event that contributed to the break-up of the Beggarstaff partnership: the bright prospect of lucrative poster designing careers for Pryde and Nicholson had already begun to fade. Many manufacturers had continued to express reservations about 'artistic' posters, and on 19 September 1896 a contributor to *Punch* had commented that such posters no longer yielded an adequate return to the artist. It had been expected that the Westminster Aquarium exhibitions would continue, but the show that took place in the spring of 1896 proved to be the last. There was even talk of the poster boom coming to an end and, before 1896 was out, the Beggarstaffs began to look around for other means of earning money. Pryde toured the provinces, supplementing his income from art by making occasional appearances on the boards; Nicholson tried his hand at commemorative prints before going on to produce a series of *Alphabet* cuts for William Heinemann the publishers [52].[42]

So, by the time the results of the *Quiver* competition were announced, Pryde and Nicholson were active in other fields. However, they had not entirely lost interest in making posters, and were mortified when their *Quiver* entry actually disappeared in transit after leaving Cassell's premises at the end of the competition. The artists clearly attached importance to this design, and in 1899 they asked Hiatt to print an appeal for information on its whereabouts. However, it is clear that a number of their contemporaries already regarded the partnership as at an end. The passage in praise of the Beggarstaffs' achievements that Clement Shorter wrote in the 8 December 1897 issue of *The Sketch* reads almost like an obituary: 'It is not too much to say that, very silently and without intrusion these two young artists were the most potent factors in that tremendous revolution of the poster in England which, during the last five or six years, has been making so singular a progress.'

Tony Drum

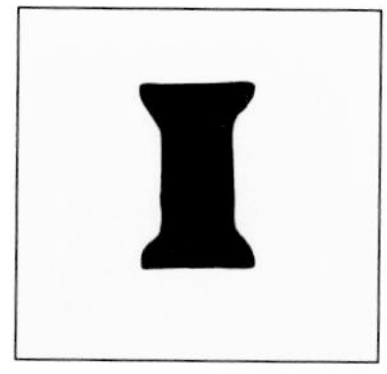

If they had ceased to think of themselves as full-time poster designers, Pryde and Nicholson were still keen to collaborate in other areas from time to time. In May 1898, for example, they sent a jointly painted *Girl on horseback* to the First International Society Exhibition in London; and about the same time they collaborated on the illustration of Edwin Pugh's *Tony Drum*, a novel about a deformed boy from a poor Thames-side district of London.

52 William Nicholson, *B for Beggar*. Hand-coloured woodcut from the de luxe edition of *An Alphabet*, 1898. The *Alphabet* series, begun in the autumn of 1896, contains a number of portraits of Nicholson's contemporaries. The point of the punning reference to the beggar's staff (Beggarstaff) in this portrayal of James Pryde seems to lie in the fact that it is the indigent artist's sole means of support.

Tony Drum, published by Heinemann in October 1898, was advertised as a book illustrated by 'J. & W. Beggarstaff'. It was not then uncommon for the illustrations in one book to be divided between two or more artists, and *Tony Drum* contains five full-page portraits by Pryde [53] and five full-page narrative scenes by Nicholson. The collaboration was thus of a different nature from that close co-operation which had produced the poster designs, for neither artist contributed to the illustrations drawn by his partner. Although the pen was the favoured drawing instrument of most illustrators at the time, the Beggarstaffs both chose pencil and brush when working on Pugh's book.

55 Will True, *Posterdom Caricatures, No. 1 – Beggarstaff Bros.* Drawing in *The Poster*, August–September 1898.

The design for the book's cover, which is blocked in dark blue and black [54], was provided by Nicholson, who produced a number of cover designs in 1898 and 1899, and who had much more experience in this area than Pryde.[43] Heinemann was one of a number of innovative publishers who had begun to recognise the importance of pictorial cover designs as a means of promoting sales of books, and Nicholson brought all his skills as a posterist to the task in hand. The *Tony Drum* cover exhibits greater graphic freedom than is found in any of the posters on which Pryde and Nicholson collaborated, but it has something of the simplicity and the harmonious integration of image and lettering of the Beggarstaffs' work. The window motif recalls the Beggarstaffs' fondness for patterned backgrounds. The possibilities of a grid formed by glazing bars as a compositional device fascinated Nicholson in particular at this time, as may be seen from a photograph for which he posed at Woodstock [frontispiece]. Will True parodied the obsession in a caricature published in the August–September 1898 issue of *The Poster* [55].

An opportunity to compare the two men's contributions to Pugh's novel is provided by their respective representations of the book's hero [53, 54]. According to the text, Tony Drum, a tiny, deformed miracle of a boy, had a 'great shock head, obliquely set between high pointed shoulders, a thick humped body, and rickety legs. His face was white and wistful, with a wonderful breadth of brow, but tapering sharply to an elfin chin. His eyes were smoke-coloured, large, deep, questioning. His mouth was pinched and wry. He could not walk upright, but shuffled onward, with his long arms dangling limply and his face to the ground.' As a designer of eye-catching book-covers, Nicholson could hardly be faulted, but his conception of Tony Drum cannot be compared to that of Pryde, who had an instinctive sympathy for picturesque low-life figures.

The existence of two quite different images of Tony Drum – one angelic, the other quite sinister – must have confused Pugh's readers; and J. & W. Beggarstaff also exposed themselves to criticism where respect for the narrative was concerned. 'I fancy,' mused Macfall in the 15 October 1898 issue of *St Paul's*, 'that it will be objected that the artists have not illustrated details of the story . . .' This indeed proved to be the case. 'At one moment,' wrote a reviewer in the *Athenaeum* of 12 November 1898, 'the Drums are almost literally in the gutter, the next they appear in the light of rather respectable and even God-fearing folk. If these are imaginary discrepancies, and we have misread Mr Pugh, it may be because we have been ourselves misled by the brilliant and untrustworthy vagaries of the Beggarstaff Brothers. Their illustrations on this occasion display them as certainly blind guides to a possibly blind reader. They profess to represent the Drums and their social *milieu*, yet give no impression of either. Instead of helping to put one in touch with the personalities of the family, the pictures add to the difficulty of focusing them. As pure caricature of the abstract sort they may be clever; but what are they doing in this book? In age, sex, feature, and general

53 James Pryde, *Tony Drum*. An illustration from Edwin Pugh's *Tony Drum: a Cockney Boy*, 1898.

53

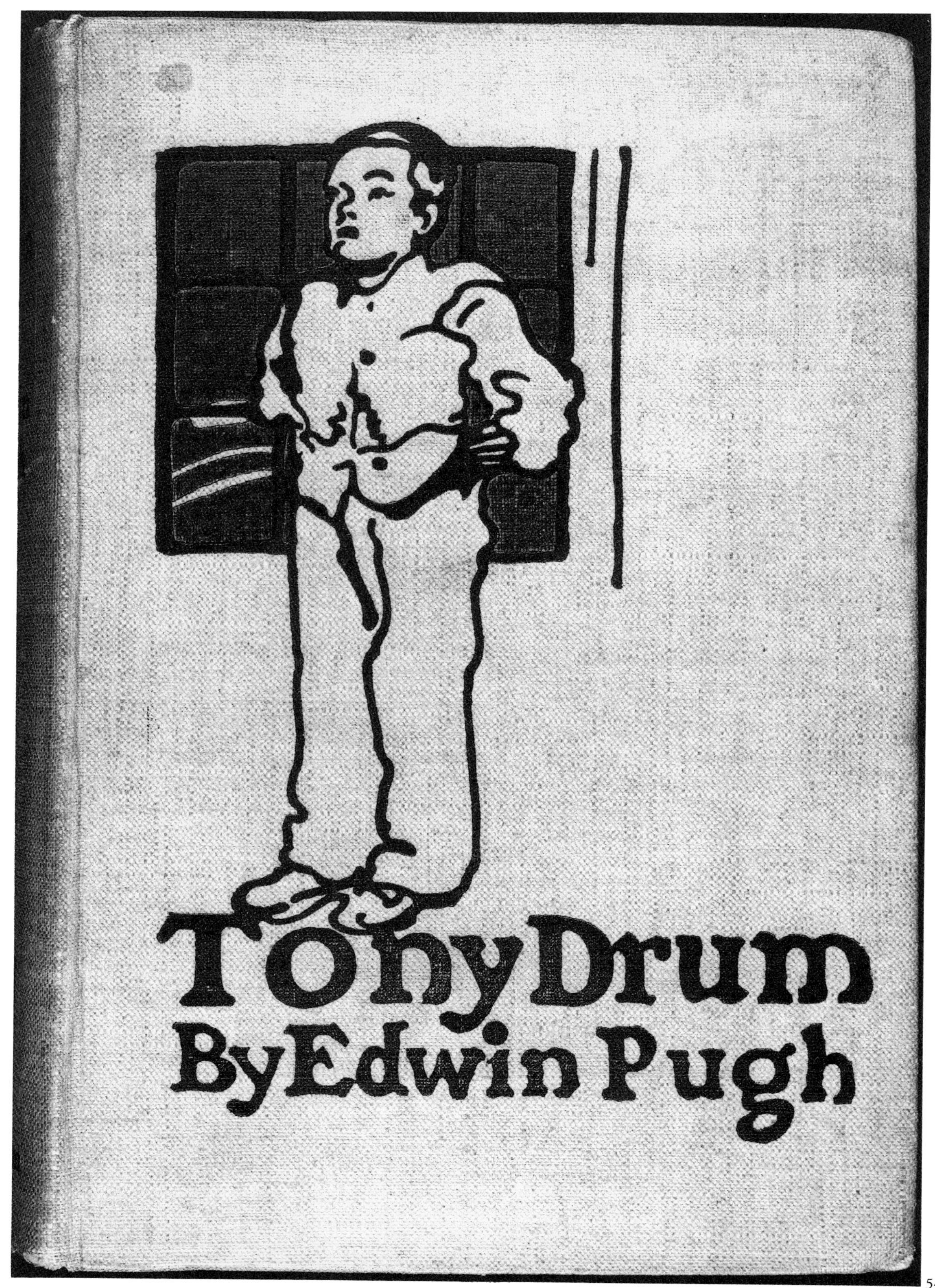

54

appearance they do not in the least tally with the descriptions in the letterpress. They are conundrums rather than Tony Drums, and remain unsolved and inexplicable.'

Other projects in the field of book illustration were discussed, notably an ambitious plan in which Pryde and Nicholson were to collaborate as writer and illustrator. Some time after Nicholson's move to Woodstock in Oxfordshire, which took place about 1898, Pryde arrived at his brother-in-law's new home full of a murder story he was writing. He wanted Nicholson to illustrate his book. Nicholson made a drawing, but Pryde's story was never finished, and in the end the project came to nothing.[44] An echo of this aborted scheme can perhaps be found in *The Murder House*, a painting by Pryde from 1905 which is now in the Whitworth Art Gallery, Manchester.

Signboards

MORE FRUITFUL AREA OF COLLABORATION THAN BOOK illustration proved to be that of painting signboards, an art form that offered much of interest to two artists who were attracted by the native simplicity and strength of popular English art.

The painting of signboards was an activity in which a number of eighteenth-century artists such as Hogarth, Richard Wilson and George Morland had engaged. Nineteenth-century artists also painted signboards (David Cox, 'Old' Crome, Millais and Birket Foster are examples), but with distinctions between 'fine' and commercial art becoming more prevalent, they did so with less enthusiasm. Constable's reaction in 1829 to a request to paint a 'Mermaid' sign for a Warwickshire inn was the typical response of an artist of standing to what had come to be regarded as a demeaning activity. However, the publication of Larwood and Hotten's *History of Signboards* (twelve editions between 1886 and 1907) contributed to a revival of interest in this popular art form, and it was not long before the humble signboard became an object worthy of discussion in both popular illustrated papers and serious art magazines.[45] Among the artists who, as a result of this revival, turned to painting signboards during the closing years of the century were Charles Ricketts, Charles Shannon, Walter Crane and William Strang.

The Beggarstaffs recognised that the problems presented to the artist by panel paintings of this kind were similar to those presented by posters.[46] Like a poster designer, a painter of signboards must take account of the fact that his work will be viewed out of doors in the full light of day. Like a poster, a signboard must

54 William Nicholson, cover for Edwin Pugh's *Tony Drum: a Cockney Boy*, 1898.

possess a harmonious combination of image and lettering that is capable of both catching the attention of the passer-by and providing him, in an instant, with a digest of information. Just as poster designers, therefore, could learn (as Pryde and Nicholson did) from what was termed in the 1890s the 'grandfather of the poster', so the painter of modern signboards could learn from the hoardings.

SIGNBOARDS ARE NOT, OF COURSE, QUITE THE SAME AS POSTERS, as Max Beerbohm observed in an essay first published in 1899. The signboard's function, wrote Beerbohm, 'is not like the poster's function, merely to arrest the casual eye and proclaim a ware, but rather to attract and fascinate one, and to make one, haply, enter the shop it overhangs. Thus is all scope given for a more delicate technique, a subtler fancy. Mere masses of colour, crude intensity of conception, wherewithout posters fail, were quite unnecessary, were inappropriate.'[47] Speaking, perhaps, as an observer of the precarious fortunes of his friends Pryde and Nicholson, Beerbohm advised modern artists to apply themselves to this 'new source of honest pennies'. Signboards, he asserted, were far more congenial to the talents of artists. 'No painter of distinction ever succeeds in doing posters. Unable to rid him of his own knowledge, he cannot learn the rather harsh conditions that they impose. But the signboard is a ground for his very own work.' The Beggarstaffs took Beerbohm's advice, and this traditional art form was to prove a useful halfway house at a time when both artists were relinquishing posters and returning to their easels.

The earliest of the panels that the Beggarstaffs are known to have painted may be the now lost sign for the Goat tavern in Kensington – a commission which probably dates from 1896 or 1897, the years in which the two artists rented a studio in that part of London. Several of the Beggarstaffs' contemporaries mention this signboard, which is described by a writer in the November 1898 issue of *The Dome* as 'amusing'. Unlike Pryde, who was not in the least interested in animals, Nicholson frequently took animals as subjects, and it is therefore likely that he was chiefly responsible for this particular work. Although no description of the sign has been traced, it is just possible that it bore some resemblance to the *Toilsome Goat* in Nicholson's *Square Book of Animals* [56]. The cuts for this series of illustrations for children were not published until 1899, but they were begun as early as 1895/6. The fact that Nicholson rarely bothered to invent a new image when an old one would do increases the likelihood of a connection between signboard and woodcut.

In 1897 or 1898 the Beggarstaffs painted an attractive signboard for the Black and White Gallery, a shop in Piccadilly founded by Louis Meyer in the summer of 1897 for the purpose of selling original drawings by the best English and Continental artists. In the late 1890s, originals by such draughtsmen as Phil May, Dudley Hardy, Cecil Aldin and James Pryde could be purchased at Meyer's premises. The Beggarstaffs' original sign for this establishment no longer exists, but a collotype facsimile [57] was made at a relatively early date, presumably at the instigation of the proprietor. This facsimile, which measures 19 × 26 inches, provides a reproduction of the original panel that is accurate enough to show the rather inexpert retouching (in the region of the lady's hands) that was done at an

56 William Nicholson, *The Toilsome Goat*. Lithographic reproduction of a hand-coloured woodcut, *The Square Book of Animals*, 1899.

57 Reproduction of a signboard painted by J. & W. Beggarstaff for the Black and White Gallery, London, 1897/9.

early date. The work, which was clearly created in emulation of Bonnard's *Revue Blanche* poster [22], shows a fashionably dressed couple studying some drawings. The subdued colour scheme and the linear character of the design relate in an appropriate way to the contents of Mr Meyer's shop.

The *Coach and Horses* [58] could be the last of the Beggarstaffs' signboards. This relatively large panel (it is nearly 3 feet 6 inches high) survives today in its original frame. Like the *Black and White Gallery* panel, it is painted in muted colours. Since there is no image on the reverse of the panel, the work must originally have been designed for attachment to a wall, but whether that wall was the wall of an inn must remain open to question. Certainly it does not appear to have been used in this way, as the paint surface exhibits little evidence of weathering. The 'J. & W. Beggarstaff' signature (above the centre of the arch) is in the form that is found in the artists' posters and designs for posters from 1894 and early 1895; but the lettering recalls that used by Nicholson around 1900. The style, which is painterly and individual, also suggests the hand of Nicholson around the turn of the century. The conception as well as the execution seems to be Nicholson's, for the coach and four is almost identical to the coach and four that Nicholson included as an illustration of the month of August in his *Almanac of Twelve Sports* (1898), and the monumental arch through which the coach is about to pass recalls similar motifs that Nicholson introduced into his work between 1900 and 1905.

58 J. & W. Beggarstaff, *The Coach and Horses*, c. 1900/5 (panel; $41\frac{1}{2} \times 34\frac{1}{2}$ inches). *Private Collection.*

60 J. & W. Beggarstaff, *Robespierre*, 1899 (design for a poster; 86 × 80 inches). *By courtesy of the Board of Trustees of the Victoria and Albert Museum, London.*

ROBESPIERRE

N THE EARLY PART OF 1899, REHEARSALS WERE UNDER WAY AT the Lyceum Theatre for *Robespierre*, a drama in five acts by Victorien Sardou that vividly recalled the Reign of Terror. Ellen Terry created the costumes for the production [59]. According to Pryde, Miss Terry remarked that if he and Nicholson produced a design for a poster advertising the play she would show it to Irving.

59 Bernard Partridge, *Henry Irving as Robespierre at the Lyceum Theatre.* Drawing in the *Illustrated London News*, 22 April 1899.

Pryde and Nicholson must have had doubts about the wisdom of responding to this suggestion: in the two years since they had sent their entry to the *Quiver* competition they had given little thought to designing posters; and in any case Irving had shown no real interest in their work in the past. In the event, however, the Beggarstaffs decided to go ahead with the project. That they did so says a great deal for Miss Terry's powers of persuasion and for the two men's belief in the extent of the actress's influence over Irving. Perhaps they felt that they now knew what Irving looked for in a Lyceum bill. Certainly they were tempted by the possibility of fulfilling, at last, their principal ambition as designers: the creation of a poster for a contemporary drama.

The Beggarstaffs' design [60] appears to have been begun before *Robespierre* opened at the Lyceum in April 1899, and it probably therefore dates from around the same time as a woodcut portrait of Irving that Nicholson made for his *Twelve Portraits* (1899). Using black and brown paper pasted on a white (but now brownish) background, the artists produced a collage measuring about 7 feet in height. The full-length figure of Irving that dominates the design is thus life size. As in some of their earlier designs, the artists represented the figure in isolation, without a background. The work is similar in some respects to the *Rowntree's Elect Cocoa* poster, but the use of shadow and the greater fluidity of line create a softer, more pictorial effect. Other differences – such as the breadth of the black masses, the nearly square format and the heavy border – reflect the influence of woodcuts made by Nicholson between 1897 and 1899. The artists were clearly at pains to make the lettering as well as the pictorial motif as large as possible, and some of the letters are superimposed on the image in order to achieve this. Today the design is something of a physical wreck, but the formal beauty of the work is still breathtaking.

Two important differences between this poster and the *Don Quixote* seem to reflect the Beggarstaffs' determination not to repeat past mistakes: the *Robespierre* design includes both Irving's name and his face. The fact that Irving's name is as prominent as the title of the play is a reflection of the actor's celebrity. But it is also a reminder of his vanity: as George Bernard Shaw observed, Irving regarded a play as merely something which was necessary for his presence on the stage. So far as the artists' portrayal of Irving himself is concerned, the work is more successful than the *Becket* and *Don Quixote* designs. Care was taken to delineate, as accurately as possible, Irving's facial features, even though this acted as a constraint on the graphic freedom that is evident elsewhere in the work. The portrait also conveys something of the actor's 'gaunt spare frame, his jerky strides';[48] and there is perhaps even a hint of the compelling stage presence that enthralled playgoers. If the Beggarstaffs failed to capture anything of the actor's personality, they could hardly be faulted for that. Like others before them, the artists found that while it was easy enough to paint Irving's elegant profile, the inner man was more elusive. Perhaps in fact the exterior was the most that one could ever hope to capture: those who knew Irving discovered that he was spiritually almost empty, with nothing behind the handsome mask.[49]

Irving, returning to the stage after illness, had only a few years to live. However, the first night of *Robespierre* on the 15 April 1899 had all the glitter and emotion of an authentic Lyceum première,[50] and Irving's performance was received by the public with great enthusiasm. Sadly, the Beggarstaffs were denied a share in the glory. When Ellen Terry broke the news that the two young artists were about to bring him another of their efforts, Irving shook his head mournfully and exclaimed 'No more mills!' In later years, Pryde ruefully recalled that the great man never looked at the *Robespierre* design. The impact of this latest disappointment may easily be imagined: the Beggarstaffs' career as poster artists was finally at an end.

Epilogue

AY 1900 SAW THE OPENING OF THE INTERNATIONAL Advertisers' Exhibition at the Crystal Palace, London – an event described in the July 1900 issue of *The Studio* as perhaps the most exhaustive and representative poster show ever organised in England. The Beggarstaffs not only sent three posters[51] and one unidentified design for a poster to this show, but they sat, along with artists like Dudley Hardy, John Hassall and Cecil Aldin, on the exhibition's art committee.[52] In March the following year the Beggarstaffs sent a further design (*Robespierre*) to the Poster Academy and the International Advertisers' Exhibition, also at the Crystal Palace.

The impression given by all this is that the Beggarstaffs were still actively involved in poster designing, but this was, of course, far from being the case. As we have seen, the continuity of the Beggarstaff partnership was threatened as early as 1896, when Nicholson began a period of intensive print-making that was to last for about three years. Nicholson was so busy making woodcuts in 1897 that he might well have been glad to forego, at that time, any further collaboration; and it was probably mainly due to Pryde that the partnership remained intact. Pryde, who enjoyed the status and celebrity he had acquired as one of the Beggarstaffs,[53] remained dependent on the partnership a good deal longer than Nicholson. While Nicholson's development to artistic maturity accelerated between 1894 and 1896, Pryde remained – inwardly at least – in a state of

61 J. Beggarstaff (James Pryde), *Caricature of Will True*. From a reproduction in *The Poster*, August–September 1898. True was a poster designer whose work occasionally shows the influence of the Beggarstaffs.

63

Clever Bill
5/ net
by William Nicholson
a New sort of Book for Children
Published by Heinemann's

64 William Nicholson, poster for *Clever Bill*, 1926. The publication advertised was a picture book for children written and illustrated by Nicholson.

65 Hoardings outside the Alhambra Theatre, London, in 1899. Non-pictorial advertisements were still common at the end of the century, and posters which do incorporate images reveal the prevailing conservative taste of advertising managers.

EXTRACT OF BEEF & FLUID BEEF
TABLE SALT
TABLE SALT
ON AND OFF
SMOKE
ALLEN & GINTER'S
Richmond Gem
CIGARETTES
SPORTSMAN
CRYSTAL PALACE
TWICE DAILY
GREAT EASTERN
TO THE SEA SIDE AND THE BROADS
CHEAP
FROM LONDON
AVENUE THEATRE
REVUE
1899
HAYMARKET THEATRE
EVERY EVENING
THE MANŒUVRES OF JANE
A GOLDEN WEDDING
LILLEY & SKINNER'S
BOOTS AND SHOES
IN LONDON
FELTOES
LEMON SQUASH
THE MOST DELICIOUS SAUCE IN THE WORLD
YORKSHIRE RELISH
STOWER'S
STOWER'S LIME JUICE
NESTLE'S
MILK
BROTHERS OF THE CHAIN
Disinfect with Sanitas
Disinfect with Sanitas
Disinfect with Sanitas
DISINFECT SANITAS
DISINFECT SANITAS POWDER
DISINFECT SANITAS POWDER
HENKEL'S
BLEACHING SODA
DAILY TELEGRAPH
ALHAMBRA
LETTY LIND
LETTY LIND
LETTY LIND
GREAT CÆSAR!
BOXES
STALLS

NOTES

1 The stencilled name seen on the sack of fodder was probably that of Frederick Beggarstaff, a farmer at Chipperfield who was also farm bailiff at Sarratt. Chipperfield and Sarratt are only a few miles from Denham. It is possible that the stencil technique that Pryde and Nicholson decided to use in their first posters was suggested by the lettering on the original Mr Beggarstaff's sack of fodder, or by some other product of nineteenth-century agricultural stencilling machines.

2 Edward Craig, *Gordon Craig. The story of his life*, 1968.

3 It is clear from the text of *Index to the story of my days* that Craig had a particular fondness for pink and grey, for he mentions this combination of colours in a painting of St Jerome by Antonello da Messina which is in the National Gallery, London (described by Craig as a painting by Bellini).

4 Lawrence Irving, *Henry Irving. The actor and his world*, 1951.

5 Uzanne (1900) related the appearance of the Beggarstaffs' *Becket* to figures in stained glass windows.

6 Beardsley's portrait of *Irving as Becket* was published in the *Pall Mall Budget*, 9 February 1893.

7 Hand-written note at the end of Ellen Terry's copy of Dr David Pryde's book, *The Highways of Literature*, now in the British Museum.

8 H. A. Jones, *The Shadow of Henry Irving*, 1931.

9 Gordon Craig's son Edward, perhaps prompted by some remark of his father's, implied that Pryde's contributions to the development of the Beggarstaff designs may occasionally have been purely verbal (*op. cit.*, 1968). Although this is possible, Edward Craig did not produce evidence to support his statement.

10 Elizabeth Robins (Mrs Pennell) recalled that 'Pryde and Nicholson . . . would wander casually into our rooms at the end of six or eight feet of poster that they had brought to show Joseph . . .' (*Nights*, 1916).

11 Nicholson joined forces with others to create works of art on a number of occasions both before and after the period during which he worked with Pryde. An early instance of Nicholson's readiness to collaborate on the creation of works of art was recorded by his friend Ernest Ringrose, who recalled during the 1930s how he and Nicholson's cousin Clive helped the young artist with the 'ground work' of woodcuts done at Newark c. 1892.

12 Craig wrote admiringly of Nicholson's dexterity in *Woodcuts and some words*, 1924. Nicholson, Craig claimed, 'could turn from one process to another and master each in about three-quarters of an hour. So to etch, to paint in oils, to paint in water-colours, to paint on glass, to paint in tempera, fresco painting, lithography, wood-engraving, to invent new ways of making posters and invent better ways day after day, was as easy for him as it is for an all-round sportsman to turn from hockey to tennis, from tennis to polo, from polo to billiards, excelling in each, to everybody's delight and despair. Nicholson was like that; and, curiously enough, besides excelling in every branch of the technique of his art, he was skilful beyond words in handling anything where eye and hand and brain have to be in perfect control, and in absolute harmony.'

13 An illustration entitled 'How to Dance' in Nicholson's *Pirate Twins* of 1929 may contain reminiscences of the *Nobody's Candles* design. The illustration in question shows a girl in blue (not black) against a yellow background. The lighted candle throws a shadow on to the wall behind the figure.

14 Spielmann claimed that the Beggarstaffs' work sent the viewer away feeling thoroughly dejected. Charles Matlack Price, who remarked on what he called the 'mournfulness' of the Beggarstaffs' posters, wrote that they 'embody many of the best points, being strong, simple, original, striking . . . but utterly lacking in a relieving note of levity. They are grim and dispiriting, gloomy, sombre and cheerless.'

15 Brander Matthews quoted by Gleeson White (1896).

16 Letter of 17 August 1945 to someone by the name of Woods.

17 William Archer, *The Theatrical World of 1894*, 1896.

18 The exhibition catalogue *L'Affiche Anglaise: les années 90* (see Bibliography under Picon) also reproduces an example of the contents bill with letterpress additions.

19 The prominent role played by the stripes on the chesterfield recalls the patterned wallpaper that is a feature of Beardsley's showcard for the publisher John Lane.

20 Robert Nichols, *William Nicholson*, 1948.

21 Pryde and Craig are said to have talked incessantly about Dumas in 1895. In the same year, Pryde advised Craig to copy figures in etchings by Callot that the latter owned. Nicholson was also an admirer of Callot (he later acquired an example of the French artist's large *Siege of Rochelle* print).

22 The *Don Quixote* lettering was probably copied from seventeenth-century examples, for the use of the lower-case form of the letter 'u' in place of a capital 'V' is characteristic of that period. Whatever the precise date of the Beggarstaffs' source, the typeface they used was thoroughly English – a fact which added to the appeal it had for the artists.

23 The figure of £50 that Steen mentioned is an astonishing sum: the Beggarstaffs' fees, so far as one can judge, were usually much less than this. Steen is not always a reliable source, and if it were not for the records that she appears to have had before her one would be inclined to conclude that she had made a mistake.

24 G. Krishnamurti re-examined the possibility that the Beggarstaffs had represented Conrad in their *Don Quixote* in *Joseph Conrad: A letter to William Nicholson*, 1985. Krishnamurti, who assumed that Nicholson had sent Conrad a 'copy' of the poster, was unaware of the existence of the *Don Quixote* woodcut. He believed the Beggarstaffs' Quixote bore a 'distinct likeness' in appearance to the Polish writer, and pointed out that when Conrad was 14 years old his tutor branded him 'an incorrigible hopeless Don Quixote' on account of his determination to go to sea. If Nicholson enclosed a letter with the woodcut that he sent to Conrad it does not seem to have survived. Conrad's letter of thanks to the artist merely remarked that 'I like the Knight very much. You have given him a lovely face and the individuality of the horse is as engaging as that of the rider.' These words do nothing to support the view that Conrad was the model for the figure of Don Quixote; indeed, if anything, they argue against that hypothesis.

25 A. Brereton, *The life of Henry Irving*, 1908.

26 William Archer, *The Theatrical World of 1895*, 1896.

27 From 'The Newest Palace of (Poster) Art', *Punch*, 19 September 1896.

28 For example, the most noticeable feature of Beardsley's design for the cover of an 1894 edition of Dostoyevsky's *Poor Folks* is a drainpipe.

29 'The Coming Poster', *Pall Mall Gazette*, 11 June 1896.

30 Charles Hiatt, 'Pantomime Posters', *The Poster*, December 1898.

31 See Hiatt (1899).

32 William Archer, *The Theatrical World of 1896*, 1897.

33 See Trevor Haddon, 'The artistic aspect of the pantomime', *The Artist*, February 1896.

34 See David Cuppleditch, *Phil May. The artist and his wit*, 1981.

35 It was common practice at this date for pantomimes to be advertised by more than one poster. An article in the 5 February 1896 issue of *The Sketch* spoke of four separate posters being used for the 1895–6 Drury Lane pantomime, and this suggests that Pennell may not have been correct in saying that the Beggarstaffs' *Cinderella* was superseded by Hardy's. The two posters could have been displayed concurrently.

36 Hiatt, 'Pantomime Posters', *loc. cit.*

37 A. S. Hartrick, introductory text in *A collection of posters*, the illustrated catalogue of the second exhibition of artistic pictorial posters held at the Westminster Aquarium, London, 1896.

38 There is a possibility that the *Girl and Screen* is identical to the two-panelled screen referred to above as *Children playing*. However, there is insufficient evidence to prove this, and the description of the 'Girl with Screen' in the April 1896 issue of *The Studio* is inconclusive.

39 Martin Shaw, *Up to now*, 1929.

40 Quoted in Frank Millward, 'A chat with Stewart Browne', *The Poster*, April 1899.

41 Nicholson made a woodcut portrait of Lord Nelson in the autumn of 1896.

42 Nicholson's first commemorative print (a woodcut of the Prince of Wales's Derby winner Persimmon) was made during the summer or early autumn of 1896.

43 Nicholson's sole responsibility for the cover is documented in advertisements in the 8 October 1898 issue of the *Academy* and the 29 October 1898 issue of the *Illustrated London News*.

44 The episode was recorded by Steen.

45 See, for example, the article 'Old English Inns' in the August 1897 issue of the *Art Journal*.

46 The connection between the two art forms was recognised during the 1890s. See, for example, Percy Hemingway, 'Roman Signs', *The Poster*, March 1899.

47 Beerbohm's essay on signboards was first published in *More*, 1899. The inspiration for the essay seems to have been the writer's acquisition of a signboard dating from c.1805 which depicted Dick Tarlington, the harlequin, 'dancing in an avenue, with a memorial urn behind him, and a mask and a tambourine at his feet' (see a letter from Beerbohm to William Rothenstein, quoted in Rothenstein, *Men and memories, 1872–1900*, vol. I, 1931).

48 Jones, *op. cit.*

49 Jones, *op. cit.*

50 Lawrence Irving, *op. cit.*

51 *Rowntree's Elect Cocoa*, *Harper's Magazine* and *The Hour Illustrated*.

52 According to the June 1900 issue of *The Poster*, the exhibition contained a number of 'bastard imitations' of Chéret and the Beggarstaffs.

53 Pryde continued to sit on art committees after Nicholson gave this practice up. In his capacity as a noted poster artist he sat on the committee of the Poster Academy in 1901 (i.e., at the time of the Academy's first annual exhibition at the Crystal Palace).

54 Four Beggarstaff works were published in the *Maîtres de l'Affiche* series, beginning with the *Harper's Magazine* in March 1896. (One of the Beggarstaff works reproduced in this series was, unusually, an unpublished design.) The first of several Beggarstaff works to be reproduced in *The Poster* was *Rowntree's Elect Cocoa*, which appeared in black and white in the June 1898 issue of this journal. The first Beggarstaff work to be reproduced in colour in *The Poster*

was the final version of *Don Quixote*, which appeared in the August–September 1898 issue.

55 Speaking to Reid in 1900, Nicholson pointed out that, under the conditions of the day, an artist cannot give the time and thought necessary to produce the kind of works the Beggarstaffs created, and live. 'A good poster is almost always an expensive luxury – to the artist that is to say' were his words.

56 See *The Poster*, December 1898.

57 Siegfried Sassoon recalled W. J. Turner telling him about an artist from Rothenburg named Heinrich Dikreiter who, in 1922, had not heard of any modern English artists other than Pryde and Nicholson (see Sassoon, *Diaries. 1920–1922*, 1981).

58 Nicholson invited Pryde to contribute to the first number of the *Owl* (1919), a magazine he founded and edited with his son-in-law Robert Graves. A contribution was promised by Pryde, but it never arrived.

Catalogue of the Posters and Designs for Posters by J. & W. Beggarstaff

ELATIVELY FEW OF THE DESIGNS FOR posters made by James Pryde and William Nicholson were used commercially, and a catalogue confined to published work alone would not do justice to the range and productivity of the Beggarstaff partnership. The present catalogue thus includes unpublished designs for posters as well as printed matter.

The January 1896 issue of *The Idler* contains a reference to a 'huge collection of finished and unfinished designs' in the artists' Denham studio. Another allusion to the Beggarstaffs' industry can be found in Ranger Gull's *Figaro* article of 25 February 1897, where the walls of the artists' London studio are described as 'lined with posters'. Unfortunately, while examples of most of the artists' printed posters have come down to us, many of the unpublished designs have been lost. (If the disappearance in 1897 of the entry sent to the *Quiver* competition is anything to go by, some of the Beggarstaffs' designs began to go missing at an early date.) However, lost works of art have a habit of turning up again; and this may well happen with one or two of the Beggarstaffs' designs for posters – which were not only valued by the artists, but sought after by collectors. The present catalogue includes a number of works whose present whereabouts is unknown, and information on these items which can be gleaned from reproductions or written sources has been included wherever possible.

In his 'Note on the Beggarstaff Posters' (*The Poster*, February 1899), Hiatt attempted a list of the works made up to that date. The 16 posters and designs for posters mentioned or reproduced in Hiatt's article by no means represent the complete Beggarstaff *oeuvre*, but no subsequent publication improved on the list. Thorpe, for example, listed a mere 10 works in his article on 'The Posters of the Beggarstaff Brothers' (*Alphabet and Image*, April 1947). Steen (1943) had the advantage of having Nicholson's notebooks before her when discussing the Beggarstaff posters (and indeed the opportunity of talking to Nicholson himself), but the 10 works that she said were made between August 1894 and December 1895 were unfortunately not described by her, or even, in some cases, identified. (The present whereabouts of the Nicholson notebooks is unknown.)

The following catalogue includes some items which have not previously appeared in the above-mentioned lists of the Beggarstaffs' work, and also a number of unrecorded variants of known works. In addition to providing a comprehensive list of the posters and designs for posters, the catalogue contains new information on a number of items: details of the appearance of some lost works, information on different states of certain items, dates, etc. An attempt has been made to arrange the various works in the approximate order in which they were produced; but here it should be borne in mind that the Beggarstaffs sometimes worked on a number of projects simultaneously, and to suggest that their products always followed an orderly and distinct chronological sequence would be misleading. The problem of establishing a precise chronology is made even more difficult by the Beggarstaffs' practice of working on a particular artistic project over an extended period of time. The position occupied by a given entry may thus provide only a very general indication of the work's date.

The catalogue includes showcards or contents bills (such as *The Hour Illustrated*) as well as posters; but decorative panels, painted signboards, oil paintings, and books to which the artists contributed illustrations have been listed separately (see pp. 108–9). The *Trip to Chinatown* bill, described by some writers as a Beggarstaff poster, is the creation of a printer's hack and has been omitted from the catalogue.

The lower- and upper-case letters suffixed to the catalogue numbers distinguish between designs for posters (identified by lower-case letters) and printed matter (upper-case). The titles given are usually either the titles preferred by the artists themselves or those used by the authors of the first published descriptions. The date given for a work is the date when it is known or believed to have been completed. Following the practice of the period, measurements are given in inches. The unit on which English poster sizes were based during the 1890s was the Double Crown, or theatre-bill size (30 × 20 inches). Most English posters of the 1890s are either Double Crowns or multiples of this size.

1 HAMLET

The *Hamlet* poster 'was made for and from me' wrote Gordon Craig (letter to Martin Hardie dated 25 September 1923). Craig, engaged by the W. S. Hardy Shakespeare Company to play Hamlet during a tour of the provinces in the autumn of 1894, told Mr Hardy that he knew a 'great artist' who had agreed to make some posters showing him in this role (see the entry in Craig's diary for 27 August 1894, quoted in the writer's memoirs, 1957). In the letter to Hardie referred to above, Craig said that he got the management of his 'strolling players' to write to the Beggarstaffs. Hiatt (1899) stated that the *Hamlet* was made 'about the month of August [1894]', but Craig later recalled that the work was begun around 8 July 1894 (letter to Hudson dated 16 April 1948). Craig (1957) believed that Nicholson was largely responsible for the *Hamlet*, but he was unduly influenced by the prominent role that Nicholson played in the printing of the poster. Craig recorded in his memoirs how he brought 20 or 30 examples of the poster with him when he arrived at Hereford on 27 August 1894 (*Hamlet* was to open in Hereford on 4 September), and so the work must have been completed by that date. Martin Hardie was told by Craig that the work 'was posted up in Hereford town and other provincial places'. The *Hamlet* was the first Beggarstaff poster to appear on the hoardings. Edward Craig claimed that Hardy 'paid Nicholson the paltry sum he asked for the mere paper and half the time the job took' (*Gordon Craig. The story of his life*, 1968).

•

a HAMLET (design for a poster)

Dimensions unknown

1894

Whereabouts unknown

[9]

The present whereabouts of the Beggarstaffs' preparatory design is unknown. However, reproductions of the work can be found in the *Magazine of Art*, January 1895 (p. 117), *La Plume*, 1 October 1895 (p. 427), Hiatt, *Pictorial Posters*, 1895 (p. 239) and *The Poster*, February 1899 (p. 50). The design shown in these reproductions appears to be composed of cut and pasted paper. No signature is visible on the design, and the lettering that is positioned at the top of 1A is also absent. The fact that this preparatory design is illustrated in a *Magazine of Art* review of the first International Artistic Pictorial Poster Exhibition at the Westminster Aquarium does not necessarily mean that it was the preparatory design which was exhibited at the Aquarium: the *Hamlet* sent to the exhibition (no. 6 in the exhibition catalogue) was not described as a *design*, unlike other Beggarstaff contributions to the show. The design is in any case artistically inferior to the printed poster, and one would not therefore expect it to have been sent to the Aquarium in place of the latter. Hiatt, who reproduced the preparatory design in the February 1899 issue of *The Poster*, gave the dimensions of the work as 72 × 40 inches. However, these dimensions may have been taken from the catalogue of the Aquarium exhibition, and they may thus refer, for the reasons given above, to the printed poster rather than the original design.

•

A HAMLET (stencil)

Dimensions unknown

1894

[10]

Craig's account of the hand-stencilling of the *Hamlet* is quoted on p. 19 of this book.

The printed versions of the *Hamlet* differ from 1a in a number of respects. The figure's costume now has a cowl; one of the feet is removed; a head in profile is preferred to the earlier head in *profil perdu*; and greater weight and compactness are brought to the lettering of the play's title. It is not clear whether it was an example of 1A or 1B that was sent to the first Westminster Aquarium exhibition in October 1894.

The presence of the words 'W. S. HARDY'S COMPANY' above the figure of Hamlet identifies 1A as the version actually used as a playbill. An example of this version is reproduced in the February 1896 issue of *Pan* (p. 333). No signature is visible in the reproduction.

B HAMLET (stencil)

Dimensions vary

Signed (by hand, lower left) 'J. & W. Beggarstaff, Denham, Uxbridge'

1894

[I]

(See notes on 1A.)

Hiatt (1899) referred to a limited edition of the *Hamlet* poster. It seems likely that this limited edition post-dated the theatrical production that the Beggarstaffs' poster was originally intended to advertise, and that it was intended purely for collectors. The edition was presumably made at the time of the Aquarium exhibition, which opened in October 1894. Examples from this edition can be distinguished from those which were used to advertise W. S. Hardy's production by the absence of the words 'W. S. HARDY'S COMPANY'. The poster is a stencil with added hand-colouring on brown wrapping paper (or *papier d'emballage*, as Bella referred to it). The cap worn by Hamlet in the example of 1B now in the Ellen Terry Memorial Museum at Tenterden shows that minor variations exist between examples from the edition. The example of 1B in the Victoria and Albert Museum, London, measures $64\frac{1}{2} \times 27\frac{1}{2}$ inches, but the dimensions of other examples differ.

A single sheet facsimile of 1B measuring $71 \times 29\frac{1}{2}$ inches was published by Imprimerie Chaix, Paris, in *Les Maîtres de l'Affiche*, 1898 (plate 107). The anonymous author of an article entitled 'The Gentle Art of Cribbing' in the October 1900 issue of *The Poster* referred to an American adaptation of the *Hamlet* by Wilbur Macy Stone.

---

2 SCHOOL FOR SCANDAL

In the autumn of 1894 the Beggarstaffs produced their second poster for the W. S. Hardy Shakespeare Company: an advertisement for Sheridan's *School for Scandal*. This production, in which Gordon Craig played the lead (Charles Surface), was probably staged for the first time on 12 October 1894. The poster must have been completed by 27 September, for Craig referred to it in his diary entry for that day ('Poster of

B ROWNTREE'S ELECT COCOA
(lithograph)
38 × 28⅝ inches
Signed (lower right) 'Beggarstaffs'
1896
[X]

This smaller version of *Rowntree's Elect Cocoa* was exhibited at the International Advertisers' Exhibition that took place at the Crystal Palace, London, in May 1900 (no. 15). Hiatt mentioned the smaller of the two printed versions in passing in 'The Posters at the Advertisers' Exhibition' (*The Poster*, June 1900).

A facsimile of the small version measuring $37\frac{1}{2} \times 27\frac{1}{2}$ inches was published in *Les Maîtres de l'Affiche*, 1899 (plate 168).

21 The Quiver

In late 1896 or early 1897 the Beggarstaffs took part in Cassell's *Quiver* competition. They were not awarded a prize in this competition, which was won by Henry Holiday. (The prize-winning designs chosen from 234 entries were discussed in the April 1897 issues of *The Artist* and the *Magazine of Art*.)

a THE QUIVER (design for a poster)
Dimensions unknown
1896/7
Whereabouts unknown

The appearance of this design is not recorded in any reproductions, but Hiatt (1899) provided a brief written description. The design, Hiatt said, 'represented a man in black tights with an orange feather in his hat on a green background'.

The design was never used commercially. According to Hiatt (1899), it 'disappeared mysteriously in transit after leaving Messrs Cassell's'. Hiatt reported that 'the Beggarstaffs would be glad to hear anything as to the whereabouts of this design, as it ranks among the best of their productions'. The work, if it survives, has still not come to light.

22 Robespierre

This work, probably the last of the Beggarstaffs' designs for posters, relates to a play by Victorien Sardou which opened at the Lyceum Theatre, London, on 15 April 1899 with Sir Henry Irving in the title role. Pryde recalled in his autobiographical essay that 'when . . . Irving was going to produce "Robespierre", Miss Ellen Terry suggested we should design a poster for it and she would show it to him . . .' Pryde's statement implies that the design was made before the production opened at the Lyceum Theatre, and if this is the case the work is most likely to have been made early in 1899.

•

a ROBESPIERRE (design for a poster)
86 × 80 inches
Signed (upper right) 'Beggarstaffs'
1899
Victoria and Albert Museum, London
[60]

Pryde recorded that Irving 'never looked at our [*Robespierre*] design', and so the work was not used as an advertisement. It was exhibited at the Poster Academy and the International Advertisers' Exhibition at the Crystal Palace, London, in March 1901. (See the review of this exhibition by Raymond Needham in *The Poster and Art Collector*, March 1901, p. 119, which refers to 'one clever and effective design, "Robespierre"'.)

A List of Collaborative Works (Other than Posters and Designs for Posters) by J. & W. Beggarstaff

The Beggarstaffs collaborated in a number of areas besides that of the poster, and a short list of examples from the fields of oil painting, book illustration, the painted signboard and the decorative screen is provided here. It is probable that the extent of the two artists' collaboration in areas other than poster design was greater than the works listed here indicate, and further evidence of such collaboration may well come to light in due course.

A1 CHILDREN PLAYING

Two panels, each 28 × 28 inches
Signed 'J. & W. Beggarstaff'
1895
Andrew McIntosh Patrick, Esq. [32, 33]

The combination of arcs and straight lines in this austere, two-panelled work recalls a preoccupation revealed by the Beggarstaffs in their *Don Quixote* designs – the first of which must date from the first half of 1895. The simplified forms of the children and the dark band that creates a border on the left, right and lower edges of the work link the design with the *Girl reading* reproduced in the September 1895 issue of *The Studio* – a design which must also be from the first half of 1895. Echoes of the *Girl reading* are also to be found in the highly formalised nature of the *Children playing* design. The work, which probably dates from around the spring of 1895, must have been intended as a decorative screen rather than a design for a poster. Whether the intention was to publish the design in the form of a print or use it as the basis for a painted screen is not clear.

See notes on no. 18 in the *Catalogue of the Posters and Designs for Posters of J. & W. Beggarstaff*, where the possibility that *Children playing* is identical with *Girl and Screen* is examined.

A2 THE GOAT

(?) Oil on panel
Dimensions unknown
c. 1896/7
Whereabouts unknown

The writer of the 'Under the Dome' column in *The Dome*, November 1898, wrote of 'an amusing sign over a public house in Kensington of the "Beggarstaff Brothers"'. The signboard was also mentioned by Steen (as a work done in collaboration with Pryde for a tavern in Kensington). Oliver Brown remembered 'being impressed in Kensington by the inn sign at the "Goat" on which they [the Beggarstaffs] collaborated' (*Exhibition. The Memoirs of Oliver Brown*, 1968). The panel was probably painted in 1896/7; that is to say during the period when the Beggarstaffs rented a studio in Logan Place, Kensington. Steen commented that the panel was later sold, and Hudson remarked that the work was once in the possession of a Mr William Law of Earl's Court Road. The signboard remains untraced.

A3 THE BLACK AND WHITE GALLERY

(?) Oil on panel
Dimensions unknown (probably 19 × 26 inches)

Signed (upper right) 'Beggarstaffs'
1897/9
Whereabouts unknown

This work, which has disappeared, was made for Louis Meyer, an art dealer who was the proprietor of the Black and White Gallery at 153 Piccadilly, London. Meyer's Black and White Gallery was established in the summer of 1897 (the 27 July 1897 issue of *The Graphic* referred to the fact that it had just begun to trade), and the Beggarstaffs' panel must therefore date from 1897 or later. A *terminus ante quem* is provided by the June–July 1899 issue of *The Poster*, which reproduces (on p. 262) one of an edition of collotype reproductions of the panel [57]. Although the signboard could have been made at any time between 1897 and 1899, it is perhaps more likely that it was made around the time of the opening of Meyer's premises in 1897. A commission dating from 1897 is also indicated by the fact that by the time the reproduction cited above was made the panel had weathered a good deal (the cracking of the paint surface is visible in the reproduction).

The collotype reproductions of the *Black and White Gallery* panel measure 19 × 26 inches, and it is reasonable to assume that this must have been the size of the original. It is not possible to say whether the panel was painted on both sides.

Although occasionally sold as such, the reproductions of the *Black and White Gallery* signboard are not of course in any sense original Beggarstaff works.

A4 GIRL ON HORSEBACK

(?) Oil on canvas
Dimensions unknown
1898
Whereabouts unknown

A painting by J. & W. Beggarstaff entitled *Girl on horseback* was sent by the artists to the first exhibition of the International Society of Sculptors, Painters and Gravers, which opened in London in May 1898. No information on the appearance of this painting has come to light, and the present whereabouts of the work is unknown.

A5 Cover design and illustrations for TONY DRUM

by Edwin Pugh
William Heinemann, London
(Henry Holt & Company, New York)
Crown octavo, 7¾ × 5 inches, six shillings
1898 (October)

This project is first referred to in a letter from Heinemann to Nicholson dated 9 December 1897.

The title-page of *Tony Drum* refers to 'ten coloured plates from designs by the Beggarstaff Brothers'. These ten illustrations (drawn, according to Thorpe, on coarse absorbent sugar paper with a pencil or brush) are in two distinct styles, revealing that while the book as a whole was a collaborative venture, the individual drawings were not. Nicholson took responsibility for the five narrative scenes: *Mrs Drum leaves 'The Jolly Anglers'* (facing p. 56); *The Drums go on a Jaunt* (facing p. 80); *Mrs Drum will take 'a Mite of warm Gin'* (facing p. 84); *Tony's Fyanky* (facing p. 124); and *Michael Drum fills his Pipe* (facing p. 218). Pryde provided the remaining five illustrations, which are all portraits: *Tony's Father* (frontispiece); *Tony Drum* (facing p. 10); *Tony's Mother* (facing p. 32); *Honor Drum and her Sweetheart* (facing p. 146); and *Tony's Grandfather* (facing p. 198). Pryde's *Tony Drum* illustration is reproduced in the present volume [53].

A number of the publisher's advertisements (e.g., that on p. 621 of the 29 October 1898 issue of the *Illustrated London News*) reveal that the cover of the book [54] was designed by Nicholson.

A6 THE COACH AND HORSES

Oil on panel
41½ × 34½ inches
Signed (top centre) 'J. & W. Beggarstaff'
c. 1900/5
Private Collection
[58]

The signature on this panel is in the form associated with works from 1894 and 1895, but the lettering relates in style to that used by Nicholson around 1900. Arches are frequently encountered in the paintings of both Pryde and Nicholson. The arch depicted here is reminiscent of structures found in Nicholson's work between 1900 and 1905.

The reverse of this panel bears the words 'Coach and Horses', but no image. The signboard is still in its original frame.

APPENDIX A

Extract from an Autobiographical Essay by James Pryde

When James Pryde died in 1941 the typescript of a short autobiographical article (parts of which were later published by Hudson) was found among his papers. Pryde's references to his professional association with Nicholson are tantalisingly brief and occasionally inaccurate, but they do at least throw a little light on the techniques and aims of the two artists. The paragraphs which allude to the Beggarstaff partnership and the development of poster art during the 1890s have therefore been appended below.

T THAT TIME [i.e., THE EARLY 1890s] POSTERS in England were, with two or three exceptions, anything but striking, although there were some very interesting poster artists working in Paris. For example, Chéret, who did some notable work for the 'Divon Japonnais' [Divan Japonais], and de Toulouse-Lautrec who in addition to *affiches* for the same *café chantant* did some remarkable designs of Yvette Guilbert, Jane Avril, Caudieux, and others.

Poster art in England was just being redeemed by Dudley Hardy, whose *Yellow Girl* for the Gaiety Theatre was a clever piece of work,[a] Maurice Greiffenhagen, later a Royal Academician, who did a poster for the *Pall Mall Budget*; and Frederick Walker, whose *Woman in White* really looked like an enlarged reproduction of a black and white drawing of his own. There was also Aubrey Beardsley's poster for what was then regarded as the advanced theatre in London, The Avenue. This last found little favour in the eyes of *Punch*, which, referring to it, made the suggestion "'Ave a new poster". These were oases in the desert of others designed by regular workers for various firms.

This was the condition of affairs when I decided to become a poster artist. The statement is incorrect. I should rather say when I decided to become half a poster artist. The other half was, of course, my brother-in-law, William Nicholson, who lived in Denham, Bucks. One day, when we were together, a friend told us he had heard there was going to be an exhibition of posters at the Westminster Aquarium, and we thought we would like to do some for it. Nicholson asked me to go to the country and collaborate with him in these posters.[b]

It occurred to me that it would be rather clumsy to have our two names on the sheet, and while strolling through an old stable yard I came across a rather battered sack which had probably contained grain. The name, Beggarstaff, was printed[c] on it, and I suggested that the Beggarstaff Brothers would be a more compact signature than our surnames. Not only was it a good striking name in itself, but its suggestion seemed to me sufficiently comprehensive.[d]

For the exhibition we did five or six large designs, not for any particular firm's commodity but merely for a given article to which the firm's name could be applied. Thus, we did a design for pianos, another for niggers [probably negro minstrels], and so on. We made them fairly large, for some were twelve feet high.

Posters are of course different from pictures, for while one can stand quietly and look at the latter, a poster has to attract the attention of the passer-by, who might be moving relatively quickly on a bus – even though those were the days of horse

---

a *Hardy made his* Yellow Girl *poster for the weekly magazine* To-Day. *The reference to the Gaiety Theatre probably arose from confusion between this work and the* Gaiety Girl *poster of 1894.*

b *The implication of this statement is that the Beggarstaff partnership was created for the purpose of making posters to submit to the Aquarium exhibition, rather than (as seems to have been the case) for the purpose of making the* Hamlet *poster.*

c *The word 'painted' quoted by Hudson is presumably an error.*

d *Pryde and Nicholson first signed their posters 'J. & W. Beggarstaff', later changing this signature to 'Beggarstaffs'. Unlike many critics, the artists themselves did not usually refer to themselves as 'brothers' during the 1890s, and in later years Nicholson protested against the use of the term.*

buses – or walking along a pavement, and have no time to notice details.

We decided that the silhouette treatment was the best, and it had this advantage, that it had not been done before. Moreover, it was a very economical way of producing a poster for reproduction, for the tones were all flat. To get this flat effect, we cut out the designs in coloured paper and pasted them on flat boards or paper. Tom Browne, the black-and-white artist, who was working for a printer in Nottingham at the time, told me of his delight in finding that the method was so easy to reproduce.

After the exhibition, Nicholson and I took to doing posters for actual firms on approval. We would take the design under our arms and call on the people to whom we desired to show them, but I must confess our success was small. Our appearance with these enormous rolls of paper was made the subject of a drawing by Phil May, the original pencil sketch of which I treasure, but he omitted the roll in the finished black-and-white drawing which was eventually published.

Among the tragedies of that time which, happily, we can now laugh at as comedies, was the poster of a Beefeater – a suggestive design printed in three colours, red, black, and yellow, which we thought particularly appropriate for a beef extract. We took it to the office of the firm in question and pinned it up on the wall of the very small room into which we were shown. After a while, the art editor or manager or whatever he called himself, a dear old gentleman rather like Father Christmas in appearance, came into the room; he gave the poster one glance and went out of the room without saying anything. Later, it was offered to Sir George Alexander, who had a Beefeater on the hoardings of St James's Theatre, but he did not find it suitable. Still later, that poster was redeemed by the proprietors of *Harper's Magazine*, who reproduced it freely in the United States, where it had a great success in advertising that publication. It had a similar vogue here.

Sir, then Mr, Henry Irving asked us to do a poster for him for the one-act play *Don Quixote* which he was then about to produce at the Lyceum. It represented that character on a white horse with his long lance in hand and a windmill in the background. He bought it, but it never appeared on the hoardings, for the play failed and was soon withdrawn.

When, subsequently, Irving was going to produce *Robespierre*, Miss Ellen Terry suggested we should design a poster for it and she would show it to him. Miss Terry broke the news that Nicholson and I intended to take a design to show him. He shook his head mournfully and exclaimed 'No more mills'. He never looked at our design.

Although we started as the Beggarstaff Brothers, we soon omitted the 'Brothers' and signed our work simply 'Beggarstaffs', the form in which most of the reproductions appeared. When we had attracted sufficient notice, a firm, the Artistic Supply Company, Limited, asked if we would design posters and let them submit them to various firms with a view to obtaining orders. On their suggestion, we designed a poster for Messrs Rowntree's Elect Cocoa which was accepted and duly appeared on the hoardings. Then they suggested we should do one for the forthcoming Drury Lane pantomime of *Cinderella*. During the rehearsal of the pantomime the Supply Company took it to Drury Lane and it was hung up on the stage, where it was made the subject of several jests by the comedians, one of whom was Dan Leno. It was likewise regarded by Sir Augustus Harris as something in the nature of a joke.

While it was hung up, Phil May happened to stroll on to the stage during a rehearsal, saw it, and went up to Gus Harris and congratulated him on his acumen in having secured it. The result was that Harris immediately accepted it and placed it on the hoardings. It was simply a coach in a flat red colour with the head of Cinderella with golden hair and black palings, with the word 'Cinderella' with the lettering very clear and readable. I think the poster had a distinct success.

APPENDIX B

William Nicholson on the Creation of the Beggarstaff Posters

In the summer of 1949, shortly after Nicholson's death, a brief memoir of the artist was published in Postscript to Image *(an occasional supplement issued by the publishers of* Image, *the quarterly of the visual arts), under the title of 'The Last of the Beggarstaffs'. The memoir, which is based on the reminiscences of an anonymous writer who had interviewed Nicholson during the last days of World War II, recorded Nicholson's answer to questions on how he and Pryde had set about making their posters.*

HE [NICHOLSON] SCARCELY RECALLED anything of his important part as one of the Beggarstaff Brothers. We wanted to know every detail about the partnership, but all he could say was 'We cut 'em out of paper. Outlines, y'know. Terrific size. Then we walked round and had a look at it, t'see whether we'd alter the colours. So much easier with coloured papers than paints'. And that was all. The rest had flown, and we wondered where else we might find a memoir of that great attempt to give the poster some of the splendour that Steinlen and Lautrec had given to the French hoardings . . .

APPENDIX C

'Arcades Ambo. The Beggarstaff Brothers at Home' (1896)

The following report of an interview with Pryde and Nicholson was published in the January 1896 issue of The Idler. *The article, written anonymously, is the most informative account of the Beggarstaffs and their work to be published during the period of the partnership. It throws light on the artists' reasons for taking up poster designing, their methods of work, and their artistic aims. The piece also provides information on the appearance of some now lost designs. Above all, it gives an idea of the serious approach to their work that lay behind the talented couple's good-humoured banter. Pryde assumed the role of the Beggarstaffs' principal spokesman during the conversation with the man from* The Idler *that took place over tea in the artists' Denham studio.*

ES,' SAID PRYDE, THE ELDER OF THE TWO collaborators, 'people are rather prone to imagine that, because a thing looks easy when finished, it must have been easy to do, but I can assure you that, although our posters have been criticised by purchasers in an off-handed manner, as "simple as a child's drawing", it has taken all the artistic knowledge which Nicholson and I have been able to gain to produce the results which you see.'

Pryde had just ushered my friend X and myself into a big double room, in which the artists design and construct their wonderful posters, and we were now pleasantly conversing on their past career, and learning how they became literally brothers of the brush.

'We are not brothers by blood, don't you know,' said Nicholson to X, 'but Pryde is my brother-in-law, and as we decided to work together, and did not care to sign our work with our two names, we hit upon the idea of calling ourselves the brothers Beggarstaff.'

'Why Beggarstaff?' I asked. 'It is a good name, and in the form of a signature it certainly adds to the beauty of your posters, but how did you get hold of it?'

'Pryde and I came across it one day in an old stable, on a sack of fodder. It is a good, hearty, old English name, and it appealed to us; so we adopted it immediately.'

At this point, X, who has a keen legal intellect, made some pertinent inquiries on the question of copyright. He did not wish to frighten them, but trusted they had registered the name in the usual manner; and he began to tell a story about a man who – ; but I have had some experience of X's stories, and I lightly pressed my heel upon his toes, whereat he conveniently choked over some tea. With considerable skill, I turned the conversation with an amiable demand for more cake.

At the end of the room, lighted by an intelligent arrangement of 'floats', as they are called on the stage, was exhibited the large poster which the Beggarstaffs had just completed for Sir Augustus Harris's Christmas pantomime, in which is depicted a yellow-haired Cinderella, turning her head and casting longing eyes on a red chariot, disappearing down a road lined with tall black columns.

'How did you first come to work together?' inquired X.

They seemed to find it difficult to answer this question. 'I suppose,' I suggested, 'that your views in art coincided greatly – to commence with ?'

'I don't know,' said Pryde, with some hesitation. 'It is very hard to relate, or even to trace the steps by which we grew together into our present style; as a matter of fact, our opinions on artistic matters differed widely when we first became acquainted. Isn't that so, kid?' he added, looking towards Nicholson, the younger of the two, but the married man, and father. Pryde always addresses Nicholson affectionately as 'kid'.

'Indeed it is,' said his friend, adding frankly and amiably, 'I am afraid I had very much to learn at that time.'

'Well, how do you manage to work together, then?' asked X. 'It would be interesting to know that. Does one of you supply the substance, and the other the form? I have known that method to work excellently in collaboration,' he said, looking me steadily in the face, so that I could not avoid his gaze.

But no, their methods seem to be so dovetailed in from beginning to finish, from the conception of an idea to its final expression, that we could learn nothing more exact as to their differences of feeling, than that Pryde generally uses a penknife to cut out the masses of coloured paper which form their original designs, while Nicholson employs a pair of scissors. Living intimately together in the same house for some years, and working daily together on the same pictures, they are in such thorough accord that, an idea once started, it seems to travel backwards and forwards, from one brain to the other, gradually picking up its character, until it reaches its final and perfect form. Neither would confess to having a greater power of imagination than the other, nor to possessing any quality, in a marked degree, which in the other was not equally noticeable.

'One of us gets an idea,' said Pryde. 'We talk it over, the other suggests an addition, the matter is reconsidered, perhaps shelved away for months. Finally, we draw the design very roughly with charcoal, on big sheets of paper, and then place the lines and masses in their places on the groundwork, which is generally of ordinary brown paper.'

We were much struck with this ingenious method of obtaining absolutely flat masses of strong colour, without the trouble of going through the frequent paintings necessary to obtain the requisite fineness and density.

'And how did you manage to select poster work,' said X, 'as a medium for expressing your artistic tendencies?'

The Beggarstaff Brothers looked at one another and smiled.

'At any rate,' said Pryde, 'we have a very satisfactory answer to that question. We are both intensely fond of painting, but one cannot always sell one's pictures; consequently, finding poster work remunerative, and seeing very great chances in it in England, we decided to adopt that.'

'It is a stony-hearted world,' mused X. 'I remember when I was in Paris, some years ago, I painted a Madonna and child – a beautiful picture – it was quite original, I assure you; but when it was finished I had the humiliation of seeing it on sale as a "genuine coloured print", price, with frame, ten francs.'

'Why did you not adopt black-and-white work,' I suggested, 'as most painters do, when the mare doesn't go fast enough?'

'We had thought of that; but, as you know, we have our own methods, and we can't work in the more or less conventional style which the publishers demand.'

'Then you did wisely,' I said, 'in turning to the advertisers, who are always on the look out for something original and striking, and do not object to a design being artistic, if it has the two other necessary qualities.'

'But they didn't all receive us with open arms,' said Nicholson; 'some of them expressed their unfavourable opinions with extreme frankness. One gentleman, an editor, on whom we called one day, just after he had lunched somewhat heartily, kindly went into details with us, and proceeded to measure from point to point on one of our designs with a yard rule, criticising freely as he went about his work. He warmed to his task, and his spirit chortled within him as he gaily and innocently pointed out the innumerable defects of our designs; that is to say, all the things in which they differed from other posters. By nature, to which you can bear witness, we are of an extremely amiable and forgiving constitution, but when he finally looked over his shoulder and glanced on our irritated faces –

' "Of course, I know nothing whatever about art," he said.

' "No," we agreed, grimly.

' "Nothing whatever," he added.

' "No, no; certainly not!" we hastened to admit, whereat he desisted from his endeavours to explain his views, and invited us to shake hands, which invitation we were not constrained to accept.'

'Name?' I queried, briefly.

But the Beggarstaff Brothers have bad memories.

'Nor, I presume,' said X, lighting one of his excellent cigars, 'was that a unique case? The artistic temperament is not best suited to the advertising of its own productions.'

'Quite so. Naturally, as we are extremely careful in our compositions, we pay particular attention to their reproduction. One of our earliest things, this design of a Chinaman, was mutilated by some idiotic imitation Chinese lettering, placed all round it to form a border; of course, it threw the design completely out, and spoiled the poster altogether.'

'That reminds me,' said I. 'I have heard especial comment made on your lettering. In the "Harper" poster it is half the design.'

'Yes,' said Nicholson. 'We have made a great study of it, and we draw and place it as carefully as any part of the design.'

'Perhaps you will tell me,' I suggested, 'what you think of French poster designers?'

'One man we admire,' Pryde replied, quickly, 'and that is Lautrec. He is one of the few artists who understand what a poster is and should be.'

'And as to English and other designers?' said X.

'We can hardly criticise them in a conversation like this,' they said.

Above our heads was a huge collection of finished and unfinished designs, in large rolls, many of which they took down and opened up for our inspection; among them the Becket design, the original of the *Hour* poster, and an odd, powerful thing representing a galloping Roundhead. Some of their designs are here reproduced from original drawings, which they were good enough to make, to illustrate this interview.

'There is one thing you mustn't forget to mention,' they said, 'and that is the great help we have received from dear old Phil May, one of the kindest and best friends we have had throughout.' They then showed us a book-plate designed for Mr May, and engraved on wood by Mr Nicholson. It is worthy of note that in everything that these two artists touch, they are extremely original; in their black and white work, their methods are either quite new or are novel applications of methods formerly in vogue. I have shown some of Nicholson's work to artist after artist, without coming across one who could tell the exact method of its drawing or reproduction.

'In our paintings, as you can see,' said Pryde, 'we work on quite dissimilar lines. This was very obvious in the joint show which we held not long since. I don't think either of us belongs to any particular school; Nicholson certainly does not; but if I claimed any at all, it would be the Glasgow school, as Guthrie, Walton, and a few others, were the first to notice and appreciate my work; and while I was staying at Edinburgh I received visits from many of them, who called to compliment me on the work which I was then exhibiting in the Royal Scottish Academy.'

To return to posters. The Beggarstaffs showed us the original of the fine poster they did for Wills's play, 'Don Quixote'. This was purchased by Sir Henry Irving; but it has not yet been reproduced. It has not been Sir Henry Irving's custom to advertise his plays by means of posters, but certainly if he were inclined to depart from his practice, he could have no better excuse than this powerful poster, representing a bare-headed knight on horseback. It is as striking to the eye as any theatrical design I have seen; and it is as refined and artistic as it is powerful.

'Here,' said the brothers, 'is a portrait of Her Gracious Majesty;' and they exhibited a fine design, in a quiet subdued style, of Her Majesty dressed in street costume, and wearing a quiet little bonnet.

'Ah,' said X, 'that is something quite apart from the usual style of portrait – to which one ever loyal magazine has accustomed us – of the Queen fondling a royal baby, or sitting in uncomely splendour on a gorgeous archiepiscopal throne, studded with huge rubies, emeralds, sapphires, and diamonds.'

'How do you like this?' asked Pryde, producing another formidable brown paper roll, and displaying an excellent design of a girl on a sofa. Like all their work, it was sheer suggestion; a young lady of a singularly graceful and delicate type of beauty, sits reading a book, on a couch powerfully striped in red and white. This design, which to the editor of the 'Studio' is the Beggarstaffs' best work, has been unjustly condemned as representing a morbid, French type. As a matter of fact, the type and character are as thoroughly English as the Beggarstaffs themselves.

Strange as their treatment of subjects is to British eyes, even the man in the street – resentful as he may be of the fact that they paint their characters flat, and not round, as he sees them – is held to stop, to throw back his head, and to admit there is something wonderfully striking about the posters which are now becoming the rage.

Tempora mutantur! Picta et mu—&c., &c.

What more can we say of two young designers? A man who elects to devote his life to art, unless he be as mendacious and rascally as our ever-interesting and admirable Benvenuto Cellini, or as quarrelsome and eccentric as Burrows, must be resolved to cause no strong excitement in the heart of the sensational interviewer, nor to impart that prickly, but not unpleasant feeling, to the scalp of the adventure-loving public. There is as much romance in an artist's life as there is in that of a man of business. To make a good artist, provided the original character and tendency are present, as in very many they are, the hardest work and most careful study are necessary. When the Beggarstaffs are labouring on a design, they make no ado about working night after night until the morning looks in at their windows, across the frozen fields. And so it must be with nearly all good artists. Though a man may not work unless he have the fit upon him, when the inspiration comes he must work till he drops.

It was hard to discover, from their own admissions, the individual tastes and characters of the two artists; but it is easy to describe their personal temperaments and appearances. Pryde, tall, good-natured, stoical; Nicholson, nervous, anxious, and intensely sensitive. They form an excellently-sorted couple; like a tall Taffy (but one more able), and a little Billee (but one not priggish), they live and work together in as good comradeship, and with as close an affection, as Du Maurier's lovable painters in their Paris studio.

I have hardly found time to describe their charming Uxbridge cottage, with its quaint, out-of-the-way staircases, impending beams, and unsuspected foot-falls for the unwary. Let it be said that most artists' studios are not as artistic as the outsider would expect; but the Beggarstaffs do not fail us here, the whole house is an artist's home from the top to the bottom, and nothing else.

On one of the walls, by the by, Nicholson showed us a most quaint and charming picture, which an affectionate father alone could devise; a print of his little boy's pretty foot in lampblack on white paper, and hung in an honourable place.

Before the rumbling old cab dragged us down long, dark, winding lanes back to the station, the four of us stood by the window, and raised our glasses in the air.

'To the Brothers Beggarstaff,' said I, 'life and success.'

'Here's to you,' said they.

'And here's to you,' said X.

APPENDIX D

'Private Views. No. 24 – The Beggarstaff Brothers', by Ranger Gull (1897)

Ranger Gull, an acquaintance of Pryde and Nicholson, captured something of the two artists' exuberant high spirits in an article published in the 25 February 1897 issue of Figaro. *The penny weekly for which Gull wrote was not the place for a serious discussion of the Beggarstaffs' work, and the article is of interest today principally for its description of the interior of the artists' large studio in Logan Place, Kensington. The article is illustrated with drawings the Beggarstaffs made of each other.*

IN THE MIDDLE OF A WALLED GARDEN AT Kensington stands a lofty building of red brick, which looks rather like a church with the spire left out. It is, as the Beggarstaffs informed me the other night, not a church but only the studio of an artist or, to be correct, of two artists.

People who make posters must have space in which to view their productions, hence the size of the work-room in Logan Place.

At one end of the hall – for it is really a big hall – stands a little black piano whose keys have often been pressed by the fingertips of ladies and gentlemen who are, as Max Beerbohm would say, 'Public People': at the opposite end hangs a great oil picture of a gentleman resplendent in trunk hose and flowing locks, which I thought was a portrait of Van Dyk, but which Mr James Beggarstaff said was 'a little thing of himself in fancy dress', though I fear the artist was wilfully endeavouring to mislead me.

If to this *mise-en-scène* you add a huge table, a bureau and two dilapidated chairs, the Beggarstaffs' studio is before you. I have been in a good many studios, but never before, I think, in one where there were neither easels nor pictures. The walls are lined with posters in various stages of completion, and the Beggarstaffs work at them perched in curious attitudes on immense step-ladders, for as the younger brother remarked 'To do posters you must be an acrobat as well as an artist.' This seemed interesting and I relentlessly made my hosts go through a little performance for my benefit, illustrating the difficulties and dangers incidental to the making of a poster. When, after various attitudes and poses, the Beggarstaffs both stood together on the extreme top of a shaky green ladder and drank my health out of the same glass, I begged them to come down to the world and then the interview commenced on the proper and recognised lines of that great art.

The appearance of my friends is too well known to need any detailed description – and besides are not their pictures here before you? – so it will suffice to say that Mr James is endeavouring to revive the old-fashioned stock and that he always appears with that uncomfortable but curious looking adornment.

'Where did you begin?' I asked them, 'or rather where did you study?'

'Simultaneously came the answer 'In Julien's studio in Paris. We came together to London and at once began to produce.'

'What was the first big thing you did?'

'They were all big,' said the younger of the brothers, 'indeed some of them measured 120 by 112.'

'I meant your first success . . .'

'Oh! I see – well the first success was our Harper's poster – that Beefeater on the wall there – wasn't it, Jimmy?'

'It was, and then came Don Quixote for Irving and Cinderella for Augustus Harris. Our latest thing is the poster for Rowntree's Cocoa, which is already out in the provinces and which London is to see very soon.'

I asked if either of them did any other artistic work beside posters, and for answer was shown some delicate pastels by the elder brother, and a series of wonderful wood-block engravings printed in three colours, done to illustrate an Alphabet for Mr Heinemann. They were very amusing. 'T' I noticed, stood for Toper, and in the picture the erring gentleman was represented leaning against a table.

'Where there's a swill there's a sway,' said Mr James.

The whole series was delightful, but in expressing my approbation and murmuring something about 'original' I secured one of those raps over the mental knuckles that sometimes come in the way of even a journalist.

'Originality,' said Mr James Beggarstaff, 'is after all only a plagiarism from nature, although a looking-glass is a better artist than Herkomer – I beg that you will appreciate without criticism for you evidently know nothing about art.'

This was crushing, and having no retort I vaguely tried to assimilate the point of the remark and then asked whom they thought the greatest artist in their own particular line.

'Lautrec!' they shouted at me, in perfect time and with the precision of a pistol shot, 'Lautrec!' and rushing to the piano

James Beggarstaff struck some resounding chords to the name of the master and then – so transient is artistic excitement – rattled away into that undignified but popular song, 'They're coming on again!' which, as these bewildering artists explained to me, was not only better and holier when sung in falsetto, but more piquant.

After that reminiscences of Paris followed as a matter of course, and I only wish I could print them. When even stories of the Quartier Latin failed us, we talked 'Art' and systems and were unseasonably serious. The Brothers like individuality in artistic work and yet, though to some critics their posters at first appeared fantastic, their work is the natural expression of the art within them and has not the slightest taint of decadence. William Beggarstaff was particularly angry at the new fads in art that are for ever cropping up and being received with acclamation. 'The sham of yesterday,' he said, 'is always taking an alias and calling itself the art of the future – then people worship.'

'Hark! Hark! the critic does bark,' quoted the other Brother, tucking in the loose end of his stock which had crept into disorder during the Paris stories – 'still you're right, there are too many people producing now who have the habitual consciousness of being very young and very interesting – it all bores me very much.'

The day was growing older and I consulted a watch which I have, whose vagaries supply a healthy irritant to its master, and at a late hour, when the Earl's Court Road was silent and the wind sang mournfully outside the studio windows, I rose and went, as I was closing the door catching a glimpse of the Brothers. They had drawn the two chairs to the fire, and with their feet on the fender and the refreshments hard by on the table, they were intensely enjoying a moment of physical ease.

APPENDIX E

'The Blind Beggarstaff of Bethnal Green', by Richard Morton (1899)

The following verses by a song-writer of the 1890s parody a well-known Victorian ballad called 'The Beggar's Daughter of Bednall Greene' (1865). The theme of blindness in the original ballad ('It was a blind beggar, had long lost his sight . . .') is adapted by Morton to tell the tale of a mud-spattered figure in the Beggarstaffs' Rowntree's Elect Cocoa *poster who is prevented (by the mud in his eye) from noticing the arrival of a bill-sticker who is about to cover him with an advertisement for Bass Beer. The 'maid of the prancing knee' who suffers the same fate is the female in Hardy's* Gaiety Girl *poster of 1894 [7]. The ballad was first published in the 12 January 1899 issue of the* Westminster Gazette.

A splotch of mud on a Beggarstaff Man,
A splotch and that is all:
But it blinds the eye of the Cocoa Man
On a Bethnal Green dead wall.

That fair, blue eye with the big, black rim,
Under the wide white frown,
Sees not the churl that pastes the bills,
The churl that tears them down.

O face with an eye that is all obscured,
O master whose work is done,
'Tis best that thou at last are blind,
O Pride of a Nicholson.

For there is thy Dudley Hardy girl,
Thy maid of the prancing knee,
Thy rouge-cheek'd lady with long bow lips,
And their promise of What-Might-Be.

Thy dainty lass of the delicate air,
With the slight, uncertain shoon –
She'll be blotted out of Bethnal Green
By a porous plaster soon.

The paste-pot fiend from his ladder leans,
Craned o'er like a young giraffe,
But, courage, Man with the darkened orb,
Lean on thy beggar's staff.

And sigh no more for the fringe of lace,
The free and wanton pose,
One sweep of the brush, and dead for aye,
Is the crimson of her clothes.

O cocoa man . . . thy sands are run,
Thy day draws dark. Alas!
The paste-pot churl in sections brings
The label of the Bass.

And o'er the splotch that shatters thine eye,
A yellow-red sheet is spread;
O Cocoa Man of the few fine tints,
Though buried, thou art not dead.

APPENDIX F

'On The Wall: A Poster Dialogue', by Richard Morton (1900)

This piece of gentle satire was published in the September 1900 issue of The Poster. *The dialogue referred to in the title takes place between a 'Beggarstaff Man' (the principal figure in the* Rowntree's Elect Cocoa *poster of 1896) and a 'Dudley Hardy Girl' (the young woman in the 1894* Gaiety Girl *poster for the Prince of Wales's Theatre [7]). Morton highlights the contrast between the vivacity of Hardy's posters and what was seen at the time as the sobriety of the Beggarstaffs' work.*

Scene: A hoarding, anywhere in London or the Provinces

Dramatis Personae:

A Beggarstaff Man

A Dudley Hardy Girl

Time: Daybreak

Beggarstaff Man:
Good morning, sweetheart!

Dudley Hardy Girl (yawning):
Morning, old sobersides.

Man: There you are, gay, frivolous, and irresponsible as usual.

Girl: You talk just as grimly as you look.

Man: And you, my dear, kick just as skittishly as you speak.

Girl: I don't believe you like my kick. Not that I really blame you, for it is a little angular, and liable to put my knee out of joint.

Man: There's a kicking sister of yours down the street, opposite the lamp-post.

Girl: Ah, she tried to put my *nose* out of joint. She's a Hassall girl.

Man: Any relation?

Girl: Not even a distant connection. But, I say, you haven't told me how I look this morning.

Man: You know my opinion. I think you look just as bright and gay and lively and brilliant as ever.

Girl: Four adjectives, and before breakfast, too!

Man: My breakfast is always with me.

Girl: Always that eternal cocoa?

Man: Always. You know I'm such a Puritan. Otherwise I should feel inclined to find you a fifth adjective and say, as is usual with you and your sisters, you look –

Girl: What?

Man: Wicked.

Girl: I'm sure I don't look anything of the kind. I may look tempting.

Man: It's the same thing, dear.

Girl: Really, now, if you did not look such a praise-God-barebones kind of individual, I should say you were a hoary old hypocrite, regretting the lost opportunities of a wasted youth.

Man: Then I should plead not guilty. I never had any opportunities to neglect.

Girl (aside):
What are you doing now, you solemn old fossil?
(*To the man*):
Oh! dear, this is an awfully tight skirt to kick in!

Man: I have often fancied that your frock somewhat limited your actions.

Girl: Papa always dresses us too tightly for anything; a lot of flounce and a fleece of lace, but such tightness round the limbs.

Man: I can't make any such complaint.

Girl: No, you are all collar.

Man: And cocoa, dear; put that in.

Girl: And hat.

Man: And white. There's plenty of white about me.

Girl: Too much blank altogether.

Man: Pray allow me to correct you. That is one of my greatest recommendations. The blank space is my special beauty.

Girl: You conceited old scarecrow. Well, I never!

Man: No, I don't think you ever did.

Girl: That's a most inconsequent observation.

Man: I feel inconsequent this morning.

Girl: In consequence of what! – if I may make such an awful musical-comedy joke.

Man: I have recovered properly from the shock your cousin gave me.

Girl: You mean Miss Price?[a]
Man: Yes, that is the lady. The one with the palette in front of her.
Girl: Ah, poor girl, that is all she has to wear. It must be very trying to her complexion.
Man: It was more trying to mine, when she stood by my side in the public highway. She hasn't been out much lately, I think?
Girl: Very little, poor dear. Anyway she's much better at home.
Man: I had a violent attack of palpitation of the heart the morning she first appeared in our society. Our Quaker acquaintance[b] –
Girl: The gentleman with the porridge?
Man: Yes. He fainted away solidly, and came quite unstuck.
Girl (with a sudden shriek): Oh! you horrid brute!
A billposter has commenced to spread paste over her.
Man: Leave the young lady alone. How dare you? Oh! dear, dear, these brutal human beings have no feelings at all. I wish I could make them understand.
Girl: Help! Help!
Man: The fiends! If they could hear me I would use language totally unbefitting a Puritan and a Beggarstaff. Oh, dear, dear!
Girl sneezes violently as the billposter spreads a yellow 'mustard' bill[c] across her.
Man: Be brave, my precious. You have not lived in vain.
Girl: But to die thus – choked by a yellow abomination! Good –
Her face is finally covered, during a paroxysm of sneezing hysterics.
Man: Good-bye, my sweet comrade. But yet a little while and such a horrible death will not be possible. Ugh! (*shudders*) Choked to death by a mustard bill! It is worse than a 'Belle of New York' Yankee atrocity. Let me sink to sleep under some of Rhead's swirls,[d] or a Baumer cyclist, and then my end will be peace!
Breaks out in hectic spots and dies in violent convulsions as the billposter smears over him a monstrosity in the shape of an impossible athlete stretching a Sandow Chain.

a *'Miss Price' is a reference to the female in Julius Price's 1895 poster for* An Artist's Model *at Daly's Theatre, London. This woman's figure (and especially her bunions) was much criticised.*
b *The cheerful figure to be seen on advertisements for Quaker Oats.*
c *One of John Hassall's designs for Colman's mustard.*
d *The arabesques that characterise the posters of Louis J. Rhead.*

Bibliography

HE FIRST ARTICLES OF ANY IMPORTANCE to be published on the Beggarstaffs were Arthur Fish's 'Another word on the poster' (*The Studio*, September 1895) and Charles Hiatt's 'Note on the Beggarstaff Brothers' (*The Poster*, February 1899). Nearly half a century after the partnership was dissolved, James Thorpe attempted to list its products in his 'Posters of the Beggarstaff Brothers' (*Alphabet and Image*, April 1947), and Derek Hudson published some interesting extracts from the autobiographical fragment that was found among Pryde's papers after his death (*James Pryde, 1866–1941*, 1949). With the exception of Judith Bronkhurst's '1895: the Beggarstaffs' "annus mirabilis"' (*Journal of the Decorative Arts Society, 1890–1940*, 1978), little else of note has been published on the Beggarstaff posters.

The bibliography printed below is not a list of texts used in the preparation of this book: many of the writings on the Beggarstaffs are short items of limited critical and documentary value. However, it is appropriate in a study of this kind to provide a comprehensive list of texts which refer to the subject in hand, and this is what has been attempted. The bibliography is confined to published texts, and the emphasis is on English language publications. Works not devoted exclusively to the Beggarstaffs (e.g. general surveys of the history of the poster) have usually been mentioned only if they make more than passing mention of the artists. Publications consisting solely of illustrations (such as the *Maîtres de l'Affiche* series of 1896–1900) have been omitted, although an exception has been made of Edward Penfield's interesting anthology *Posters in Miniature* (1896). Entries in encyclopedias and biographical dictionaries have not been included.

Publications have been arranged alphabetically under authors' names, and page numbers have been given in the case of articles.

ANON., 'Arcades Ambo. The Beggarstaff Brothers at home'. In *The Idler Magazine*, London, January 1896 (pp. 519–28). Steen erroneously refers to this article as in the *Strand Magazine*. (See Appendix C in the present volume.)

ANON., 'Palette scrapings'. In: *The Poster*, London, September 1900 (pp. 34–5).

ANON., 'The last of the Beggarstaffs'. A short memoir of William Nicholson in *Postscript to Image*, an occasional supplement issued by the publishers of *Image*, the quarterly of the visual arts, London (summer) 1949. (See Appendix B.)

BARNICOAT, JOHN, *A concise history of posters*, Thames and Hudson, 1972 and 1975.

BELLA, EDWARD, 'L'Affiche Anglaise'. An essay dated 14 August 1895 in *La Plume*, Paris, 1 October 1895 (pp. 426–30).

BREDT, E. W., 'Die Beggarstaff'. In *Das Plakat*, 15 July 1914 (the text of this illustrated article is on pp. 138–41).

BRONKHURST, JUDITH, '1895: the Beggarstaffs' "annus mirabilis"'. In *The Journal of the Decorative Arts Society, 1890–1940*, no. 2, n.d. [1978] (pp. 3–13).

BROWN, ROBERT, 'Posters at the turn of the century'. In Dawn Ades, *Posters*, Abbeville Press, New York, 1984 (pp. 14–21).

BUTTERFIELD, FRANCIS, 'Beggarstaffs' (Art in our time, no. 104). In *Courier*, August 1954.

CRAIG, EDWARD GORDON, *Index to the story of my days. Memoirs of Edward Gordon Craig, 1872–1907*, Hulton Press, 1957.

ELVIN, RENÉ, '100 years of poster design'. In *Art and Industry*, London, May–June 1951 (pp. 162–75).

FARR, DENNIS, *English Art, 1870–1940* (Oxford History of English Art, Vol. XI), Oxford University Press, Oxford, 1978 (pp. 75, 78–9).

FERN, ALAN M., Introductory text in *Word and image* (posters from the collection of the Museum of Modern Art), Museum of Modern Art, New York, 1968.

FISH, ARTHUR, 'Another word on the poster'. In *The Studio. An illustrated magazine of fine and applied art*, London, September 1895 (pp. 215–19).

GULL, RANGER, 'Private Views, no. 24 – The Beggarstaff Brothers'. In *Figaro* (new series), London, 25 February 1897 (pp. 1–2). (See Appendix D.)

HIATT, CHARLES, *Picture Posters. A short history of the illustrated placard, with many reproductions of the most artistic examples in all countries*, George Bell & Sons, London, 1895. Reprinted in 1976 by E. P. Publishing, East Ardsley (Yorkshire).
—, 'A note on the Beggarstaff Brothers'. In *The Poster*, London, February 1899 (pp. 44–53).

HILLIER, BEVIS, *Posters*, Weidenfeld & Nicolson, London, 1969, and the Hamlyn Publishing Group, Feltham (Middlesex), 1974.

HUDSON, DEREK, *James Pryde, 1866–1941*, Constable, London, 1949.

HUTCHISON, HAROLD F., *The poster. An illustrated history from 1860*, Studio Vista, London, 1968.

JACKSON, HOLBROOK, *The eighteen nineties. A review of art and ideas at the close of the nineteenth century*, London, 1913 and later editions.

KOCH, ROBERT, 'The poster movement and "Art Nouveau"'. In *Gazette des Beaux Arts*, Paris, November 1957 (pp. 285–96).

'M.', 'The poor man's picture gallery'. In *St Paul's*, London, 2 March 1895 (pp. 412–3).

MACFALL, HALDANE (writing under the pen name 'Hal Dane'), 'The art of the past year'. In *St Paul's*, London, 5 January 1895 (p. 12).

—, 'Some thoughts on the Brothers Beggarstaff'. In *St Paul's*, London, 5 October 1895 (p. 11).

—, 'On Posters'. In *St Paul's*, London, 11 April 1896 (pp. 62–3).

—, 'On posters – II'. In *St Paul's*, London, 18 April 1896 (pp. 111–12).

—, 'On some illustrations by the Brothers Beggarstaff'. In *St Paul's*, London, 15 October 1898 (pp. 98–9).

MACFALL, HALDANE (writing under his own name), 'The work of James Pryde'. In: the *Magazine of Fine Arts*, August 1906 (pp. 231–7).

MALHOTRA, RUTH, and THON, CHRISTINA, *Das Frühe Plakat in den Europa und den U.S.A.* (vol. I – *Great Britain and the United States*), Gebr. Mann Verlag, Berlin, 1973.

METZL, ERVINE, *The poster: its history and its art*, Watson Guptill Publications, New York, 1963.

MORTON, RICHARD, 'The Blind Beggarstaff of Bethnal Green'. In the *Westminster Gazette*, London, 12 January 1899 (See Appendix E.)

—, 'On the wall. A poster dialogue'. In *The Poster*, London, September 1900 (pp. 12–13). (See Appendix F.)

PENFIELD, EDWARD (foreword by Percival Pollard), *Posters in miniature*, John Lane, London, and R. H. Russell & Son, New York, 1896.

PENNELL, JOSEPH, 'Angleterre'. An essay on English posters dated 25 September 1896 in M. Bauwens, T. Hayashi, La Forgue, J. Meier-Graefe and J. Pennell, *Les affiches étrangères illustrées*, G. Boudet, Paris, 1897 (pp. 29–76).

PICA, VITTORIO, "A travers les affiches illustrées: II, Angleterre'. In *L'Estampe et L'Affiche*, Paris, 1898 (pp. 178–84).

PICON, GENEVIÈVE (introduction), *L'affiche anglaise: les années 90*. Catalogue of an exhibition held at the Musée des Arts Décoratifs, Paris, between June and September 1972 (compiled by Laurence Bosse, Anne Kimmel and Dominique Negel). Musée des Arts Décoratifs, Paris, 1972.

PRICE, CHARLES MATLACK, *Posters. A critical study of the development of poster design in continental Europe, England and America*, George W. Bricka, New York, 1913.

PRYDE, JAMES, unpublished typescript of a short autobiographical article (n.d.) found among the artist's papers after his death in 1941. Extracts from this typescript are quoted in the biography of Pryde by Derek Hudson. (See Appendix A).

REID, J. A., 'William Nicholson and his work'. In *The Art Journal*, London, March 1900 (pp. 72–7).

ROGERS, W. S., *A book of the poster*, Greening & Company, London, 1901.

ROTHENSTEIN, JOHN, *Modern English Painters. Sickert to Smith*, Eyre & Spottiswoode, London, 1952.

ROWLANDS, STANLEY, 'Masters of the poster: II – The Beggarstaff Brothers'. In *Commercial Art*, London, March 1931 (pp. 115–20).

RUTTER, FRANK, *Art in my time*, Rich & Cowan, London, 1933 (pp. 18, 45–8).

SIMMONDS, FLORENCE, 'William Nicholson, Painter'. In *The World's Work*, January 1907 (pp. 125–33).

SINGER, HANS W., 'Plakatkunst'. In *Pan*, Berlin, February 1896 (pp. 329–36).

SPARROW, WALTER SHAW, *Advertising and British art. An introduction to a vast subject*, John Lane, London, 1924.

SPIELMANN, MARION H., 'Posters and poster-designing in England'. In *Scribner's Magazine*, New York, July 1895 (pp. 34–47). This article was also published in Arsène Alexandre, M. H. Spielmann, H. C. Bunner and August Jaccaci, *The Modern Poster*, Charles Scribner's Sons, New York, 1895.

STEEN, MARGUERITE, *William Nicholson*, Collins, London, 1943.

THORPE, JAMES, *English illustration: the 'nineties*, London, 1935.

—, 'The posters of the Beggarstaff Brothers'. In *Alphabet and Image*, London, April 1947 (pp. 33–47). Reprinted in 1975.

UZANNE, OCTAVE, 'William Nicholson et son art'. An essay dated 29 October 1897 in William Nicholson, *Almanach de douze sports*, Paris, 1898 (pp. 5–16).

—, 'William Nicholson'. In *Art et Décoration*, Paris, March 1900 (pp. 90–6) (An abbreviated, English language version of this article was published in *The Book Buyer*, New York, in 1901).

WHITE, GLEESON, 'The poster and its artistic possibilities'. A paper read to the Society of Arts on 14 January 1896 and published in *The Journal of the Society of Arts*, London, 17 January 1896 (pp. 168–79).

WREDE, STUART, *The Modern Poster*, Museum of Modern Art, New York, 1988 (p. 15).

Acknowledgments

HE AUTHOR IS GRATEFUL TO MRS ELIZABETH Banks for permission to reproduce copyright material in this book. Thanks are also due to the following for permission to reproduce photographs of works in public collections: the City Art Galleries, Leeds; the Ellen Terry Memorial Museum, Tenterden; the Kunstgewerbemuseum, Cologne; the Museum für Kunst und Gewerbe, Hamburg; the Museum of Modern Art, New York; the National Gallery, London; and the Victoria and Albert Museum, London. The photograph of Ellen Terry and Edward Gordon Craig in *Nance Oldfield* was supplied by the Raymond Mander and Joe Mitchenson Theatre Collection, and the photograph of posters outside the Alhambra Theatre by Aerofilms. Colour transparencies of the Beggarstaffs' *Chinaman* and *Rowntree's Elect Cocoa* were generously provided by Emmett Publishing Ltd, who photographed the works in question during preparation of *British Posters in the Victoria and Albert Museum*. (This publication reproduces on colour microfiche all the museum's posters from 1851 to the present day, and is issued with a *Summary Catalogue of British Posters* by Margaret Timmers.)

INDEX

Principal references are in bold type.
References in square brackets are to illustrations
(roman numericals refer to colour plates).